THE KNIFE EDGE OF EXPERIENCE

THE KNIFE EDGE OF EXPERIENCE

Rosemary Haughton

Darton, Longman & Todd

First published in Great Britain in 1972 by
Darton, Longman & Todd Limited
85 Gloucester Road, London, SW7 4SU

© 1972 Rosemary Haughton

ISBN 0 232 51175 6

Printed in Great Britain by
Latimer Trend & Co. Ltd., Plymouth

Contents

Acknowledgements

THE author records her thanks to the publishers of the following copyright works, from which she has made quotations: To William Heinemann Ltd. and Harper Row, Publishers for *The Edwardians* by J. B. Priestley; to Miss Sonia Brownell, Secker and Warburg Ltd. and Harcourt, Brace, Jovanovich, Inc. for *The Road to Wigan Pier* by George Orwell; to John Farquharson Ltd. for *The Story of the Amulet* by Edith Nesbit; to *New Blackfriars* for *Notes from the Underground* by Daniel Berrigan; to Faber and Faber Ltd. for the poem *Carnal Knowledge* from *Fighting Terms* by Thom Gunn; to M. B. Yeats, Macmillan and Co. and the Macmillan Company of New York for the poem from *The Collected Poems of W. B. Yeats*; to Routledge and Kegan Paul Ltd. for the poem from *The Collector and Other Poems* by Peter Redgrove; to the Estate of the late Mrs. Frieda Lawrence, Laurence Pollinger Ltd. and the Viking Press, Inc. for the poem from *The Complete Poems of D. H. Lawrence*; to Sheed and Ward Ltd., London and Sheed and Ward, Inc., New York, for *In the Redeeming Christ* by F. X. Durwell, C.SS.R.; to Darton, Longman and Todd Ltd. and Doubleday and Co. Inc. for *The Jerusalem Bible* and to Darton, Longman and Todd Ltd. for *Theological Investigations*, Volume I, by Karl Rahner, S.J.

1. The Theology of Experience

THE "theology of experience" is an impressive phrase; it sounds concerned, relevant—all the right things. And it really is the right thing for it means, essentially, a realization that a healthy and living theology must grow out of actual experience and cannot thrive if each generation of theologians busies itself with separating yet more strands of speculation from the yarn spun by the previous one. But talk about the theology of experience can be misleading, and indeed liable to turn very quickly into the usual pseudo-theological mutual back-scratching sessions that happen all too easily at conferences and other gatherings of intellectual Christians, if they allow themselves to suppose that they are discovering something new. The fact is that *all* good theology is, and always has been, a theology of experience. To explore the idea now is to be thoroughly traditional in the proper and necessary sense, and therefore to break new ground. For the true Christian, theological tradition requires that we constantly break new ground—the ground being man's experience of God at work in his life, which has a different impact in every age. People experience it differently according to the way particular cultures live, and think about themselves. Experience drives us continually to new ways to express what God is doing to us. The theology of experience is as new as next week and as old as man.

In order to assist an understanding of how this works I have chosen a handful of examples, at random, from the past. With the knowledge gained from seeing how our forefathers drew their theology from their experience of living it may be easier to see how we must discover God at work in our own generation, in the personal and communal experiences which we feel are unique to our time.

One of the most effective ways of getting a religious group to think hard about theology is for something to happen to them that contradicts their religious beliefs, or which seems to. For the Jews, their crushing defeat and the ignominious exile of large numbers of their nation was such a contradiction, for they had always assumed that their status as God's chosen people entitled them to his constant protection, and guaranteed final victory and prosperity. Temporary setbacks, famines and other disasters might occur as chastisement for unfaithfulness, but the wiping out of the nation as a nation, the total loss of sovereignty and the destruction of every symbol of past power and future hope—that was definitely not part of the usual theological picture. The prophets who watched or survived the disaster explained it as the result of Israel's pride and unfaithfulness, but there is quite a large element of hindsight about this. Nothing quite so thorough in the way of chastisement had really been envisaged beforehand. So when, after a time, it became possible to hope for a return and a remaking of the people, a remarkable change had taken place in the religious thought of the people and their leaders. This can be described very simply as a broadening of the notion of God's will and plan. His people could think of their own destiny as a key part of something much greater than their own national history. The inclusion of foreigners in God's design was not a new idea, but whereas in earlier times it had seemed that Israel's development and greatness was Yahweh's primary concern, while other peoples might be brought to share their privileges in some measure, after the exile there is a consciousness, among the more thoughtful at least, that although Israel's election is central to God's plan the meaning of that election is not as obvious as had been thought and Israel's role is not necessarily that of top dog.

This change was a spiritual and theological deepening without which the full revelation of God's plan in Jesus would have been meaningless, and it happened because a disastrous experience enforced it. So we find the deutero-Isaiah talking about Cyrus, a gentile, in terms that give him a theological role almost comparable in importance to that of Moses himself—and one Jewish tradition actually compared him to Abraham. He is called by Yahweh (Isa. 41: 4) and no-one in Israel was wise enough to foresee such a possibility—"No-one predicted it, no, no-one proclaimed it", yet "from the rising sun I summoned him by name" (Isa. 41: 25–26). Cyrus is called the "anointed" of Yahweh, who has "taken him by his right hand"; he is God's "man of destiny", and finally his "beloved", of whom he says, "I, yes I myself, have summoned him, brought him and prospered his plans" (Isa. 48: 34).

The words which the prophet puts into the mouth of Yahweh at this point are the perfect exposition of what we mean by the theology of experience, and they provide the rationale for the use of events as theological sources: "Come near and listen to this; from the beginning I have never spoken to you obscurely, and all the time these things have been happening, I have been present." The wise men of Israel had experienced the "things that have been happening" and had listened to the revelation of God which was contained in them. Their theology was indeed a theology of experience and there followed the great theological flowering of post-exilic Judaism, which led directly into the theology of the New Testament.

The theology of Jesus is also, throughout, a theology of experience—it is the experience of God's fatherly love, made evident in Israel's past and also in everyday life. Because Jesus spoke "with authority" he often presented the conclusions of his theology without demonstrating its sources in experience—he himself was the experience which provided the evidence for his words. But sometimes we find him giving little lessons in theological method, indicating how we are to discern the nature of God, and his will for man, by noticing how ordinary people behave. The implication is that God "has been present" in quite ordinary "things that have been happening" as well as in great national crises, and that he is to be attended to there. So the lesson of God's endless forgiveness is drawn from the behaviour to be expected of an ordinary father, and God's will that the sick should be healed on the Sabbath is deduced from the practical behaviour of any sensible man who owns an animal. "But he said to them, 'If any one of you had only one sheep and it fell down a hole on the Sabbath day, would he not get hold of it and lift it out?' " (Matt. 12: 11–12). We are so accustomed to the parallel drawn by Jesus between the action of the owner of the sheep and the will of God for a sick man that we may not notice what it means—our own spontaneous impulse to care and help tells us something about God, and something about our own nature as God's creatures. We should notice that this is not like the Kingdom parables, which illustrate God's actions by analogy. This is a reference to experience, and the reference implies that we can actually listen to God when we observe human events and reactions in the right way.

St. John's gospel (16: 25–31) shows the same thing, but in almost the opposite way, in the discourse at the Last Supper. The very fact that what Jesus is saying can only be believed on his authority—since no-one can verify his statements about something that only he can know—is taken as evidence that he is what he says he is: "we believe that you came from God". The logic behind this apparently illogical reaction is that the disciples already have an experience of Jesus which assures them that he is truthful and utterly trustworthy. When he explains things to them in metaphors, they know he is expressing, in terms they can comprehend, matters which, in their fullness, must be beyond their comprehension. So when he makes direct, simple and quite unprovable statements about himself, they find this reassuring. John shows him speaking not out of, or to, *their* limited experience, but purely out of his own, and they know he speaks truly.

My last example from Scripture is different again, and perhaps the most radical in its implications. Paul's problem with the Galatians was that they were allowing themselves to be persuaded by Judaizers that their experience of conversion and freedom in Christ was not sufficient; they must also keep the old Law. Paul's answer to this (3: 1–5) is an appeal to their own personal experience. On this occasion he doesn't tell them what is the case, though he was not noticeably reluctant to invoke his own authority when necessary. He asks them to judge the matter for themselves, because he has no doubt whatever of the outcome, if they honestly answer his question: "Was it because you practised the Law that you received the Spirit, or because you believed what was preached to you?" Having asked that question, and knowing what the answer must be, he goes on to support and reinforce the conviction it must bring, by elaborate exegesis and theological argument. But the appeal is first to experience, the rest comes to elucidate what is already known, though perhaps not recognized. And this appeal to experience remains valid for us, even if we non-Jews find the supporting rabbinical arguments niggling and far-fetched.

The appeal to experience is constant in Christian theology, even though in many cases we may disagree with the interpretation put upon experience in particular cases. St. Thomas constantly refers his arguments to things he expects his readers to know, either from direct experience or from simple deductions from observation. Some of his references are to current beliefs which could not be tested and have since been disproved or at least dropped, but the intention is always to learn from what is verifiable. In his answer to the question, "Whether man has free will" (*Summa* 1: 9; 83: 1) he refers first to Scripture, and then to the experience of everyday human behaviour—"Man has free-will, otherwise counsels, exhortations, commands, prohibitions, rewards and punishments would be in vain. Man acts from judgement, because by his apprehensive power he judges that something should be avoided or sought.

But because this judgement, in the case of some particular act, is not from natural instinct, but from some act of comparison in the reason, therefore he acts from free judgement and retains the power of being inclined to various things" and so on. It is possible to disagree with the interpretation put on the experiences referred to, but it is clear that St. Thomas regards the reference to verifiable data as essential to the development of a sound theology.

My last example of the appeal to experience in theology is very recent, and comes from the earlier work of one of the greatest of contemporary theologians, Karl Rahner. It is particularly to the point because it is not only an example of the use of recognizable experience as a source of theological truth, but it is itself actually a statement of a principle underlying the theology of experience. It comes in his essay on the "Development of Dogma", in Volume 1 of his *Theological Investigations*. He is arguing that there is a kind of knowledge operating in the study of theology which cannot be immediately or properly expressed in dogmatic propositions, but is the basis from which propositions may eventually be developed, expressed in terms appropriate to the particular culture and time. In order to show how this works he refers to a common experience, that of falling in love (p. 63).

"Let us suppose that a young man has the genuine and vital experience of a great love, an experience which transforms his whole being. This love may have *presuppositions* (of a metaphysical, psychological and physiological kind) which are simply unknown to him. His love *itself* is his 'experience'; he is conscious of it, lives through it with the entire fullness and depth of a real love. He 'knows' much more about it than he can 'state'. The clumsy stammerings of his love-letters are paltry and miserable compared to this knowledge. It may even be possible that the attempt to tell himself and others what he experiences and 'knows' may lead to quite false statements. If he were to come across a 'metaphysics' of love, he might perhaps understand absolutely nothing of what was said there about love and even his love, although he might know much more about it than the dried-up metaphysician who has written the book. If he is intelligent, and has at his disposal an adequately differentiated stock of ideas, he could perhaps make the attempt, slowly and gropingly, approaching the subject in a thousand different ways, to state what he knows about his love, what he is already aware of in the consciousness of simply possessing the reality (more simply but more fully aware), so as finally to 'know' (in reflexive propositions). In such a case it is not (merely) a matter of the logical development and inference of new propositions from earlier ones, but of the formulation for the first time of propositions about a knowledge already possessed, in an infinite search which only approaches its goal asymptotically. This process too is an explication. Here too there is a connexion *in re* between an earlier knowledge and later explicit propositions. But the starting-point and the procedure are not those of the logical explication of propositions, which we first took as model for the development of dogma."

Rahner refers to this as an "analogue", but I think this may have been simply a prudent avoidance of provocation—the work was first published in 1954, a time when adventurous theology could still be silenced or at least hampered by busybodies whose insensitivity to real theology was only equalled by their zeal for the preservation of sacred clichés. The passage just quoted describes an experience which is not so much *analagous* to the development of theological knowledge as actually an *example* of it. You know, Rahner was saying, how human love is experienced and how propositions can be developed about it, yet there is something deeper and more—not less—true going on which is real knowledge but can never be fully and finally expressed in propositions.

This is the kind of whole knowledge which is the basis of all true theological statements. It takes a particular kind of awareness and intelligence to be able to reflect lucidly on this knowledge, and communicate it to others in such a way that they will recognize what is being referred to. This is the theologian's job, but the knowledge on which he draws is not especially his, it is available to all who have the kind of experience on which he is drawing—the experience of grace, of God at work. If his work is to be fruitful for the whole people it must grow from, and refer back to, this basic Christian awareness. A large part of the work of theology must also consist of the study of propositions drawn directly from the experience of Christians— personal, communal and historical—and of making deductions from these propositions and stating conclusions which can be usefully referred to the daily life of the Christian community, its attitudes and decisions, in the areas of both belief and morality. But none of this is valid unless it has its roots in experience, which is where, as the prophet said, God has been present.

There is one big difficulty, however, which seems likely to make the appeal to experience so unreliable as to be virtually useless except as a game for professional theologians. This is the very obvious objection that if true prophets, saints and theologians have appealed to experience as the source of their knowledge and the place where God is present, so also have the false prophets, and the preachers and founders of every heretical church and sect that ever exploded out of the ranks of a church grown smug and apathetic through loss of contact with its own basic experiences. Some of the expressions of faith once dismissed as heretical or even diabolical have now been rediscovered and at least partly assimilated into the main development of Christian thought. Others still appear distorted and inhuman. The judgements of our forefathers are not necessarily ours, and perhaps we are readier than they were to look for truth in strange disguises, just because we can recognize that the propositional form does not necessarily accurately express, let alone exhaust, the deeper knowledge. But we still cannot suppose that all appeals to experience support true statements about the nature of life, hope and God. Some judgement, some discrimination, is necessary, even if it be provisional and tentative. If theology finally refers itself to a knowledge which, as Rahner says, is "already possessed", how can we know which of the propositions ostensibly referred to it are valid and which are what Rahner calls "false statements", however sincerely proposed? What kind of approach to common experience is required in order to discern clearly how God is working among us, and what he wants of us?

These two questions are complementary. The second question gives a new direction to the first, for our problem in the present —any present—is to come to a sufficiently true understanding of God's presence in our experience for the experience to become a true guide to Christian decision. A sure and certain judgement on the validity of theological propositions drawn from experience can only emerge after a long time, probably a very long time—at least enough time for sectarian, national, social or personal emotional involvement in the experience to have dwindled to little or nothing. It is only necessary to glance at present ecumenical stalemates due to theological wrangles several hundred years old to see how long a time may be needed. But in order to live with God and preach the Gospel now we don't need the kind of matured judgement which can be expressed in measured and accurate terms guaranteed to last a few hundred years at least. We only need to be reasonably certain of the way God is showing himself to us, and it doesn't matter if we express our insights inadequately or with some exaggeration or false emphasis.

The second question, therefore, is the important one from the moral point of view—that is, from the point of view of what we do about God and Jesus today, tomorrow, and in a few years' time. But there have to be both questions, if the second is to be answered properly, because if we couldn't ask questions about the ultimate truth to experience of our propositions, the attempt to understand God's presence in experience would be

17

useless. However difficult and lengthy it may be, the task of discriminating between a true insight, and one distorted by prejudice or wishful thinking or emotional pressure, is essential. In other words, we must try to discern, and act on, our experience of God's action *now*, in such a way that at some future time we, or our descendants, may look back and say, as Jesus said to Simon, "it was not flesh and blood that revealed this to you but my father in heaven" (Matt. 16: 17). Or, as St. Paul put it, "instead of the spirit of the world, we have received the Spirit that comes from God, to teach us to understand the gifts that he has given us" (Cor. 2: 12).

What kind of spirit is this? It may help to evaluate the spirit in which we try to understand experience as God's presence if for the moment I leave theology aside altogether, and study the way in which similar experiences have been used by different people to form quite different judgements, according to the spirit in which they lived, or observed, these experiences. For this purpose I have chosen a time and a subject about which few people are likely to get very emotional nowadays. This is the class consciousness of the British middle class round about the first decade of this century. The experiences about which the four authors I have chosen are writing are very similar, and the first two, who are writing for a serious adult readership, came from almost identical backgrounds. These two are using their own childhood memories—though one is younger than the other—as part of the material from which they draw conclusions about the wider social scene and its implications. This may seem an odd and very narrow subject to choose; the reason I chose it is that it was something about which people felt very strongly, and these feelings had far-reaching social consequences, whose effects are still with us—and not only in England. In this it had the same quality as many of the contemporary issues about which our views depend a lot on personal experience—such issues as race, educational opportunity, the gap between rich and poor in our own country and also between rich and poor nations. These and others are matters in which people are emotionally involved, and which are also the kind of experience—personal, national or global—or all three— upon which we must reflect when we try to discover God's presence and its meaning for us. How we interpret his action will depend on how we experience these things.

Here is J. B. Priestley in his seventies, looking back on the social setting of his boyhood, in his expert, lucid and beautiful portrait of an era—*The Edwardians*.

". . . the lower middle-class lived in fear of sliding back into the jungles and bogs of the workers. It had achieved respectability and was terrified of losing it. What a sardonic friend of mine used to call the 'shop and chapel people' were respectable at all costs, arming themselves against any raids by the disreputable. There were of course a few genuine puritans in all classes during these years, but the respectability so prized by this lower middle class does not deserve to be called puritanism; it had not the old depth and dignity; it did not wonder what God would think but what the neighbours would think; it could never have followed an Oliver Cromwell or applauded a Milton; it was narrow, suspicious, carping, mean-souled."

After this general assessment he goes on to draw on personal reminiscence:

"Even my father, a very different type, intelligent, brave, public-spirited, could not altogether escape the infection, simply because he too had emerged, not without self-discipline and sacrifice, from a working-class background. We had a deep affection for each other, and the only sharp resentment arrived in my middle 'teens when I began to strike out for myself— coming home too late, wearing odd clothes, being seen out with girls, usually older than myself, and so forth. My father's cry then was, 'What are the neighbours going to think?' a question that did not worry me then and has never troubled me since. But my father, a schoolmaster, in spite of—perhaps because of—his advanced views, had to look respectable, getting

19

up early on Sunday mornings to put on his frock coat for Sunday school (he was superintendant) and chapel, while many of his relatives and mine (on my mother's side, and a feckless lot) were lying in and then going out, dressed anyhow, for beer."

The key sentence is the one which tells us that what the neighbours thought "did not worry me then and has never troubled me since", a claim, incidentally, which is justified by Priestley's whole subsequent career. Public opinion, approving or disapproving, has never bothered him. So he also writes with appreciation of those middle-class people who did not conform to the standards his family upheld (p. 106).

". . . I knew several 'drop-outs' and they never seemed to be having a bad time. One of them who . . . was living with a woman he ought not to have been living with, could have been comfortably off if he had stayed in the family business, but he preferred to play twice nightly in a music-hall orchestra—the fastest I remember at dodging out for a beer if he was not wanted for ten minutes. Another 'drop-out' was a descendant of a sporting squire . . . he was a railway clerk, probably earning about 35s. a week; a big jovial bachelor who never seemed to be brooding over his social decline and fall."

The mood of these passages is appreciative. It is not sentimental, he does not disguise the meanness of the middle-class ideals, and therefore of many of the people he describes, but neither is he embittered. There is no rejection, and he can admire and respect the qualities of his father even while he notices how social conformity held him in its grip. There is a sense of freedom in his writing, he is bound neither to conform to the demands of his milieu, nor to reject it. He judges reflectively, moderately, acutely and with real enjoyment of the quality of life as he encountered it.

George Orwell was born several years after Priestley, so his memories of this period are those of a small boy, not a teenager. But the milieu is almost the same, and neither the slightly higher social level which he (rather too carefully) claims, nor the difference in age, accounts for the difference in mood. Here is his account of the type of family into which he himself was born, from *The Road to Wigan Pier.*

"In the kind of shabby-genteel family that I am talking about there is far more *consciousness* of poverty than in any working-class family above the level of the dole. Rent and clothes and school bills are an unending nightmare, and every luxury, even a glass of beer, is an unwarrantable extravagance. Practically the whole family income goes in keeping up appearances. . . . A shabby-genteel family is in much the same position as a family of 'poor whites' living in a street where everyone else is Negro. In such circumstances you have got to cling to your gentility because it is the only thing you have; and meanwhile you are hated for your stuck-upness and for the accent and manners which stamp you as one of the boss class. I was very young, not much more than six, when I first became aware of class distinctions. Before that age my chief heroes had generally been working-class people, because they always seemed to do such interesting things, such as being fishermen and blacksmiths and bricklayers. . . . But it was not long before I was forbidden to play with the plumber's children; they were 'common' and I was told to keep away from them. . . . So, very early, the working class ceased to be a race of friendly and wonderful beings, and became a race of enemies . . . (p. 172) hence, at the age of seventeen or eighteen, I was both a snob and a revolutionary. . . . I loosely described myself as a Socialist. But I had not much grasp of what Socialism meant, and no notion that the working class were human beings."

The bitterness is obvious. In other parts of the book he describes his reaction against this brain-washing and his attempts to identify with the working class, though these are experiences which he recorded in more detail in *Down and out in Paris and London.* He came to hate the kind of people his family had been, but also to despise those who tried to break out of that class by themselves despising the easy targets:

" 'I'm not a snob' is nowadays a kind of universal *credo*," he wrote. "Who is there who has not jeered at the House of Lords, the military caste, the Royal Family, the public schools, the huntin' and shootin' people, the old ladies in Cheltenham boarding houses, the horrors of 'county' society. . . ." Yet one gets the impression that, although he despised and tried to get away from it, this was in fact his *own* attitude. He tried hard not to take this way out, but something prevented a real truthfulness in his descriptions of either the middle class he hated or the working class he admired. He claimed that he did not idealize the working class, but he couldn't help it. He despised the newly educated working-class boys as "very disagreeable people, quite unrepresentative of their class", at least partly because they didn't fit into the mental picture he needed to have. In one passage he described a scene which, he says "is still reduplicated in a majority of English homes", though he points out that unemployment is making it rarer (this was in the thirties). Here is his lyrical description of what he calls "the sane and comely" shape of the working man's home life; a description which is the outcome of romantic longing more than observation.

"Especially on winter evenings after tea, when the fire glows in the open range and dances mirrored in the steel fender, when Father, in shirt-sleeves, sits in the rocking chair at one side of the fire reading the racing finals, and Mother sits on the other with her sewing, and the children are happy with a pennorth of mint humbugs, and dog lolls roasting himself on the rag mat—it is a good place to be in, provided that you can be not only in it but sufficiently *of* it to be taken for granted."

But he never was. He seems never to have been able to experience the way of life he admired as *his* way of life, precisely because he would never stop hating the one he had rejected. In order to hate it thoroughly he had to keep on using working-class life as a measure of absolute value, even against his own better judgement, which warned him not to idealize. He was

never able really to love the working people he turned to, because he would not allow himself to see any good in the class he
condemned wholesale and without discrimination. Here,
finally, are two passages, one from Orwell and one from
Priestley, which register a personal conclusion drawn from
what has been observed both from personal experience and
from the recorded or recounted experiences of others. Orwell's
admits an unbridgeable gap and indirectly apportions the
blame for this with a bitter (and quite untrue) generalization
that the passage from Priestley quoted earlier is itself sufficient
to refute.

"Is it ever possible to be really intimate with the working
class? . . . I will only say here that I do not think it is possible.
. . . I have seen just enough of the working class to avoid
idealizing them, but I do know that you can learn a great deal
in a working-class home. . . . Take, for instance, the different
attitude towards the family. . . . A working man has not that
deadly weight of family prestige hanging round his neck like a
millstone . . . a middle-class person goes utterly to pieces under
the influence of poverty; and this is generally due to the behaviour of his family—to the fact that he has scores of relations
nagging and badgering him night and day for failing to 'get
on'."

Priestley makes his judgement about a whole era, because
that is what his book set out to do, whereas Orwell's aim was
more restricted. But it is apparent that this judgement grows
chiefly from the same milieu, his own, that Orwell rejected.
His book is scathing about the failures and hypocrisies of the
period, in all classes, but he was able to see other things as well.

"I do not believe I have any illusions about Edwardian
England. I was there . . . but when the last illusion has been
stripped away, something solid remains; there is that gleam of
gold in the wreck. The age somehow created an atmosphere in
which English genius, talent, generosity of mind, could
flourish. . . . The Edwardians, . . . could be quarrelsome, mili-

tant, with various aggressive sections of society bitterly opposed to one another; yet they could create and maintain that atmosphere of hopeful debate which never survived the Great War . . ." (p. 289).

My other two examples are quite different. I have often found that children's writers are extremely revealing of contemporary habits of mind, just because their aim is not primarily to preach a doctrine but to tell a story. When there is a moral to the tale it is not the conscious intention that is revealing but the incidental assumptions. So often it is the things people take for granted that reveal their true values, not the aims they proclaim. This is important for theology, because all through history unnoticed assumptions about life and society have drastically modified theological development. It is too much to expect that Christians should be so detached from the society they live in as to be able to observe these assumptions without sharing them, though a few may manage it. Orwell, the enthusiastic socialist, shows in the passages quoted how difficult it is to be uninfluenced by class-conditioned assumptions any socialist must reject. So with Christians. We are part of a larger society whose basic assumptions often contradict aspects of our faith, and we constantly adapt our faith to fit these assumptions because they are our own. My two next authors are both well known and deservedly well loved, writers for children, one English and the other an American who wrote often about England. I have chosen passages that show the authors' attitudes to class distinction and both writers show, as Orwell did and Priestley did not, a difference between conscious ideals and unconscious assumptions.

Edith Nesbit was an early socialist and feminist, but she is remembered almost exclusively for her children's books. In several, the children are transported into the past. In this passage the four children in *The Story of the Amulet* have, for a change, brought the Queen of Babylon out of the past into the present, that is to London in 1903. To entertain their visitor the children take her for a ride in a cab to see the sights of London. But what the Queen embarrassingly notices is not the buildings but the people:

"But how badly you keep your slaves! How wretched and poor and neglected they seem," she said, as the cab rattled along the Mile End road.

"They aren't slaves, they're working people," said Jane.

"Of course they're working people. That's what slaves are. Don't tell me. Do you suppose I don't know a slave's face, when I see it? Why don't their masters see that they're better fed and better clothed? Tell me in three words."

No-one answered. The wage system of modern England is a little difficult to explain in three words, even if you understand it—which the children didn't.

"You'll have a revolt of your slaves if you're not careful," said the Queen.

"Oh, no," said Cyril. "You see they have votes—that makes them safe not to revolt. It makes all the difference. Father told me so."

"What is this vote?" asked the Queen. "Is it a charm? What do they do with it?"

"I don't know," said the harassed Cyril, "it's just a vote, that's all! They don't do anything particular with it."

"I see," said the Queen, "a sort of plaything."

As an ironic comment on the hypocrisy of the democratic myth this is hard to beat, yet the same author, in another book, shows us a rather different attitude to class differences when the children (the same children) come home unexpectedly to find that the servants have taken advantage of their absence to leave the house and go on an unauthorized outing. The children get into the house, and when they find out by chance exactly where the absent servants have been they prepare a booby trap to welcome them back. When the resulting chaos subsides Cyril tries what amounts to a bit of blackmail:

"Now," said Cyril firmly, when the cook's hysterics had

25

become quieter, and the housemaid had time to say what she thought of them, "don't you begin jawing us. We aren't going to stand for it. We know too much. You'll please make an extra special treacle roley for dinner, and we'll have a tinned tongue."

When the housemaid refuses, and explains that they have been visiting her sick great-aunt, the children reveal that they know the truth of the night's outing, and the servants are properly appalled. After a while:

"Forbear," said Cyril, "they've had enough. Whether we tell or not depends on your later life," he went on, addressing the servants. "If you are decent to us we'll be decent to you. You'd better make that treacle roley—and if I were you, Eliza, I'd do a little housework and cleaning, just for a change."

The servants gave in once and for all.

"There's nothing like firmness," Cyril went on, when the breakfast things were cleared away and the children were alone in the nursery. "People are always talking of difficulties with servants. It's quite simple, when you know the way. . . . I think we've broken *their* proud spirit.'

This is all fairly harmless, and in other places in the stories the children are clearly on terms of affection with various people of working-class origin. But it is noticeable that even the worthiest of these are presented as faintly comic, though lovable. In fact this attitude is not so very far from the one held up for us to be appalled at in Frances Hodgson Burnett's *A Little Princess*. (Why this book hasn't been made into a film I can't imagine.) It dates from some years before the Nesbit one, but the social attitudes are the same. Here is the hard-hearted, intensely snobbish Miss Minchin, reacting to a request from her rich show-pupil Sara, that Becky the scullery-maid should be allowed to watch her unwrap her birthday presents.

"If you please, Miss Minchin," said Sara suddenly, "mayn't Becky stay?"

Miss Minchin was betrayed into something like a slight jump.

"Becky!" she exclaimed. "My dearest Sara!"

Sara advanced a step towards her:

"I want her because I know she will like to see the presents," she explained. "She's a little girl too, you know."

Miss Minchin was scandalized. . . .

"My dear Sara," she said. "Becky is the scullery-maid. Scullery-maids—er—are not little girls."

It really had not occurred to her to think of them in that light. Scullery-maids were machines who carried coal-scuttles and made fires.

So Becky is allowed to stay—but "not too near the young ladies". It is clear where Mrs. Hodgson-Burnett's sympathies lie, yet her reaction to a situation where girls of thirteen are "machines for carrying coal-scuttles" is confined to sympathy and to practical expressions of compassion which are purely private in character. Later in the book her heroine loses all her wealth and spends two years as a drudge in the school where she was once the show-pupil. She suffers the hardship and humiliation which are commonly the lot of the children of a group regarded as essentially inferior, and on her errands she sees in the streets the evidence of still greater misery. Yet when the happy ending comes, and her fortunes are restored, her benefactor's advice to her, when she recalls past suffering, is "try to forget it". And all Sara herself can think of to do about what she has learned so painfully is to arrange for the owner of a bakery, who was once kind to her, to distribute buns to poor children who happen to be around, and send her the bills. The same assumptions about the unchangeableness of the basic social and political situation is to be seen in the better known *Little Lord Fauntleroy*. The hero is on excellent terms with tradesmen of various kinds, and is full of compassion for the hardship he discovers on his grandfather's estates, but all that he, or the author, proposes to do about it is to remedy immediate and visible misery by personal intervention.

All these extracts refer to experiences connected with the

once explosive subject of class distinction, which is no longer very urgent to us, but they clearly tie up with questions of human value, of whether human beings are indeed equal, whether revolution or compassion is the right remedy for oppression, and whether or not these two are compatible. None of the authors I have quoted were attempting to draw theological conclusions from the experiences they remembered or observed, for that was not their concern in the books referred to, and this enables us to judge with greater impartiality, undeterred by our own theological bias, whether the kind of attitude each had to his or her subject was the kind that enabled true and human conclusions to be drawn, on which action could be based in the present, and which would stand the test of time.

Priestley is the most appreciative, the one who is open to experience in every sense, because of a kind of spiritual freedom that springs, evidently, from the warm affections, the appetite for life, and the energetic principles which informed the home in which he grew up. Yet perhaps he is almost too appreciative. His delight in all that is adventurous and hopeful in people of all kinds does not obscure his keen vision of the evil and pettiness in individuals or institutions, but it makes him less inclined to get involved in any kind of crusade. At one point in his book, describing the wreck of *The Titanic* and the monstrous folly of hubris that caused it, he does actually draw a theological conclusion, which is characteristically a warning against the human temptation to think we know, or can know, all the answers. The new awareness of ecological damage through technological idolatry only confirms his judgement. But must our theological judgements be merely negative?

Orwell would suggest the opposite. The practical suggestions in the same book for bringing socialism to pass seem, now, extremely naive, and he himself repudiated them later, but he did try to translate experience into judgements on which action of some kind could be founded. His bitterness against the evils he experienced made him intolerant and narrow, yet the blaze of his anger illuminated a whole range of social and political squalor and hypocrisy, and forced people to notice them. If his approach had been more balanced and rational he might have been less effective as a prophet.

Perhaps the differences indicate for us not a choice of one proper approach but two different types of the theology of experience—the prophetic and the reflective. Both are needed, for they balance and correct each other. Both must, if they are to be real, draw on authentic experience, and both have their dangers. In the case of the prophetic style there is the danger of narrowness and prejudice, of encouraging hatred rather than hope. There is also the danger of being confused by one's own rhetoric, so that the kingdom of heaven is narrowed down to an earthly utopia, because utopia can be conjured up in the imagination of people in need of hope, whereas the kingdom of heaven eludes imagination and is beyond the scope of immediate goals. One of the dangers of the reflective type of theology, on the other hand, is that it sees too clearly the distortions to which enthusiasm can lead. It discerns the action of God even in human beings who are misled, and distorted by worldliness, and is therefore reluctant to pass judgement on the world, until the time has long passed when judgement would be helpful to Christians seized with the need for moral decision. The prophet can act in a way which a later judgement may reject, yet he may be right to act in this way, since he must act *as* the occasion demands, *when* the occasion demands. But the reflective theologian must not be browbeaten into allowing it to be thought that the wider and slower and more emphatic judgement is unnecessary, still less an evasion of responsibility provided it, too, is a theology of experience and not of ideas, bred from each other to the point of decadence. For it is these more detached and slower judgements that help to build up the heritage of Christian moral sensitivity that makes possible the right decisions in crisis situations. The prophet is needed to

29

draw on experience and demand obedience to God, but the prophet needs to be obedient to the reflective theology of experience recollected in tranquillity, if he is to lead the people to hear the voice of God, rather than his own voice.

The spirit of a true theology of experience, then, is both enthusiastic and open, both appreciative and clear-sighted. But also it is very humble. The prophet only remains a true prophet if he humbles himself to recognize and to love the presence of God in the most humdrum and unimaginative of God's people. He fails if he values his own insights so much that he cannot love God in people who disagree with them. The reflective theologian also must be humble enough to listen to the prophet's voice even if his own approach does not lend him that kind of certainty and force. Detachment is a tool for discovering truth, not a justification for moral neutrality on questions where decision is required. And this is perhaps where the small-scale, more intimate evidence of the children's writers can help us, for they reflect the everyday actions and reactions of ordinary people, and these people are children, who often show up with uncomfortable accuracy the values their elders prefer to keep discreetly covered. What we learn from these passages is, I think, that although none of us is exempt from the influences that form and deform our particular culture this need not discourage us too much. Even Orwell's attempts to break free of his milieu were only slightly successful, and because he failed he allowed himself to despair. But there is no need to despair, or even to be ashamed of emotional and cultural bias which we cannot help, provided we recognize its existence and allow the full power of the Christian gospel to counteract it gradually. If, after all our efforts, we still stand convicted of lingering prejudices or conditioned reactions that is no great tragedy. Christ came to call sinners, not the just.

There is a reverse side to this, also. Having the right, Christian principles is no guarantee of right decisions in particular situations. "If I have the gift of prophecy, understanding all the mysteries there are, and knowing everything . . . but without love, then I am nothing at all." It is not enough to draw true conclusions from experience, we must also experience *in love*, only then shall we find the right personal balance between the demands of the present prophet and the developing tradition. Neither is sufficient without the other, either in itself, or in ourselves as we each wrestle with the theological task.

For each of us has a theological work to do. We may think we haven't but we can't help it, because every time we make a decision, or refuse to make one, we are showing whether we are with Jesus or against him. We are saying something about what we think Christianity is. There never has been a time when even the most passive could really allow a Church to make all their moral decisions for them, because the decision to obey is itself a moral decision and can have as many varied motives, from cowardice to true humility, as any other decision. Nor are the most emancipated present-day believers making their moral decisions in a vacuum. The cloud of witnesses from all ages and places surrounds them. They choose with the Church, or against it, in some sense or other, and there are many senses. So also our decisions form part of the tradition, and create the material from which others draw in making their decisions, and all these decisions depend on the kind of notions we have about what God is doing, to us and around us. Our practical decisions display theological premises, whether we like it or not. To say "I'm not interested in theology" is to display an ignorance as gross as that betrayed by people who smugly disclaim interest in politics, not knowing that every day is crammed with political acts, from greeting certain people and not others in the street, to posting letters, or buying a newspaper. Each of these acts springs from a given political doctrine, however unperceived it may be. A person may not even know the meaning of the word theology, but there is scarcely a conscious act which does not express a theological position of some kind, and even unconscious motivations often grow from the theological views of our forefathers.

No-one is exempt, but a special responsibility lies on those who recognize what is happening, as the second Isaiah did in his time. Just as God's spirit breathes through all the world, but only a few know whose breath they feel on their foreheads, so theology concerns everyone, but only a few know that. On these few, lies the responsibility of expressing a theological judgement which is sensitive to experience, truthful, and humble. We are not to be afraid of making mistakes, nor need we be cast down by them, but we are to listen, and to speak what we hear, confident that for all our faults we have the spirit of Christ.

2. The Experience of Community

COMMUNITY is a word that is used in all kinds of ways. It has a special cachet at the moment, even for people with no religion; creating community is the right thing to be on about. Sociologists discuss how it happens, anthropologists report on it, town planners wrestle with its requirements. Faced with this development of contemporary thought, Christians rush along trying to catch up, and develop theological theories to fit contemporary forms of community life with a slap-happy disregard for the finer points of the disciplines on which they draw for inspiration.

But if there have been some over-hearty attempts to leap on to the band-wagon in full career the preoccupation with community is not merely fashionable, but its fashionableness reflects its re-discovered importance. The fashion may change, indeed, it is already changing, but the need for Christians to understand the concept of community remains. And here, immediately, theology must draw on experience if it is to avoid futile idealization and the consequent expense of spirit, not quite in Shakespeare's sense but nearer to it than may be immediately apparent.

The first kind of experience which is relevant to the study of community is one through which all those now adult have passed, though most of them were not aware of it. This is the experience of cultural change, which has taken place more rapidly, and more self-consciously, in the last generation of the west than ever before. The rise of the social sciences and their increasing influence on our understanding of human life shows how concerned our society is to understand what is happening

B

to it, and it is out of this social self-examination that the concern with community has arisen. When communities are working well they don't ask themselves what makes a community work, people just assume that this is the normal way to be. When it is noticed that groupings long taken for granted are coming unstuck, that beautiful new housing estates produce neurotic or potentially suicidal people, that cities are deteriorating not only physically but spiritually, that suburban isolation is not so much a privilege as a social disease—then we start asking ourselves what is wrong. And one of the things that is discovered to be wrong is the deeply entrenched emphasis on individual development, as if a human being were something essentially autonomous. Because various forms of community living—village, street, family, and so on—had gone on for so long it was not realized how necessary a recognized pattern of relationships is to human living. It was only when the traditional patterns were broken up, and the consequences observed, that people began to worry about community. And at the same time that planners and doctors and psychiatrists were beginning to think more sensibly about town-planning the philosophers were developing ways of thinking about people that made it clear that human beings are not separate from their circumstances, that their language and their social structure is what they are, and that man can only learn himself in community. This is to over-simplify drastically, but in thoughtful hands, the sort of deep study that can be brashly summed up in this fashion has been immensely fruitful in elucidating a view of the nature of human culture of which Christians can make use in seeking to understand the contemporary experience.

But like all changes of direction in philosophy the really important and far-reaching effects of this change will be in its diffusion as a general climate of thinking and feeling, among people who are not even aware that there is such a thing as philosophy, let alone theology. The process of change in this particular case has not gone very far, but there are already a great many people, including many Christians, who have got hold of the main idea, who recognize that it is a change, and roughly from what it has changed, and who are enthusiastic about its implications without being very subtle in their appreciation of what it is actually saying. These people are often students of various kinds, including older school-children as well as undergraduates. They are also older professional people, mainly on the academic side, who are well educated and well read philosophically and theologically, but whose thinking in this field relies less on the original pioneer studies than on interpretations and applications of them. This is an important stage in altering the thinking of any culture and in providing the raw material of theological development. These people are the writers and teachers now and especially in the future, and they will influence cultural development much less by what is actually said and written in novels, textbooks, lessons, plays and poems than by the unspoken assumptions about the nature of human life and destiny that underlie their metaphors, statements and explanations.

This is how it has always been. This is how cultural change takes place. The European popular culture of the Middle-Ages, for example, was shaped by the pattern of thinking that emerged from the attempts of scholars to present and preserve Christian teaching in terms of Greek philosophy—this being the available and useful one. In the popular versions it was rationalized and streamlined until it provided fairly simple categories for talking about different types of human behaviour, about life and death and the destiny of man. But all this conscious religious language, as it became part of the language of ordinary life, was used in practice in odd ways, because in this "popular" form it wasn't nearly subtle enough to express adequately the range, richness and ambiguity of human experience. The emergence, mixed with this, of an elaborate popular lore of Christian mythology, with a certain pagan colouring, was the inevitable result. Some of this lore got

35

absorbed back again into a sort of pseudo-official Christianity, and persists even now in shadier regions of Christian doctrine like that concerned with devils, and in semi-magical attitudes to sex. In fact a popular religious culture not very firmly based on a Christian theology was gradually built up. Its conscious language began as a sophisticated theology, but was modified by an "underground language" of myth and fable expressing those aspects of life with which the official religious language was not adequate to cope, at least in a form that was suitable for common use.

At a later stage of this culture, there was an uneasy middle area, consisting of people whose way of thinking and feeling was formed by popular Christian culture, since that *was* their culture, but who were beginning to be influenced by philosophical ideas of the Renaissance at the conscious level, and had never been in contact with the subtler intellectual forms of the older culture. This is why the eighteenth century often shows among educated Christians a sophisticated rationalist philosophical attitude living alongside a traditional type of Christian mythology. The next stage, of course, is the abandonment of the older culture, and the embracing of the new ideas, but in a religious form—that is, in a form which can express a purpose and direction in a whole culture rather than just an intellectual system.

This process of turning a new philosophical system into something that can be assimilated as culture is what many Christians are involved in at the moment, whether they know it or not. It is part of the process of making a religion, and it is an essential one, but true religion can only grow from theology, drawing in turn on properly understood experience, and this is urgent, because through the agency of the kinds of people I mentioned, the philosophy of man as essentially a community creature is already trying to find appropriate religious forms. In order to do this it draws not only on the strictly intellectual formulations that originally defined what was going on, but on

36

those far less clear-cut processes, those underground languages of human need and hope and discontent, to which the philosophers themselves were reacting, like a sort of intellectual seismograph, in their own interpretations. We are engaged in the creation of some kind of religion that really belongs to and also forms the culture of our time.

This is not something we simply invent. It is partly a matter of feeling what goes on, and saying it, and partly a matter of pointing out the significance of what is going on, and trying to direct it. This religion-making, in fact, has a doctrinal and a moral aspect, as one would expect. Religion-making is not the same as developing a theology, for theology studies man's relation to God in all his experiences, and I do not mean by religion, in this context, a specifially Christian or even theistic affair. I am using the word to refer to the sort of language that expresses the sense of purpose and destiny in a culture. Religion is not simply a culture though it must fit the culture in which it operates. The culture itself is the whole way of life of a particular class, nation or tribe, and it includes those underground currents of fear and hope and inarticulate passion which cannot be fully and consciously expressed but which erupt into poetry, music and painting and make their influence felt. But a culture is to a great extent its conscious language, its self-understanding which provides the common assumptions behind all everyday activities and decisions. Religion also is a language, and it is about the whole cultural situation, but it is not simply an articulation of the given cultural situation. Religion is a language *about* the cultural situation, but it is one which relates it to its destiny, it evaluates cultural phenomena in relation to the purpose of man's life, and judges them. It has a reference beyond the cultural situation itself, although to make sense it must be a language that is clearly about the actual, known, cultural situation, and not about some other. The distinctive thing about religion, then, is its reference to something beyond the given or known situation, something which is ultimate in

37

human life, though not necessarily God. In this use of the word, the task of formulating in religious terms the newly apprehended reality of community-man is obviously a vital one.

The need to formulate the doctrine of community has been forced upon mankind by the exigencies of recent history, sometimes by problems immediate to us such as those mentioned earlier, but also by even more far-reaching changes—the growth of world population, mass communication, the sudden vulnerability of mankind to its own crimes, and the consequent need for a distribution of responsibility that is world-wide.

We now have a huge reservoir of relevant—and frightening—information about all these things, and more is emerging all the time. Yet knowing a lot of facts about the situation, and expressing them in terms of a doctrine of communal responsibility and the necessity of co-operation cuts little ice, simply because people don't operate strongly at that level. This message doesn't get through. The philosophers, driven by history, take the thing apart, reshape language and patterns of thinking to cope with newly aggressive facts and demands. People do hear, and are shaken, and the message gets through, but only to a few, and these are the ones who can understand the complexity of the process of trying to express a whole lot of new concepts in a language shaped by quite different ones, in order that a new language may become available—a fantastically difficult and contradictory task when you think about it.

If the new demands are to be met they must be realized at all levels of human living, not just at the intellectual level. This is the process of making a religion, whereby the human response that must be made to cope with circumstances is articulated in myth, and poetry, and moral attitudes and social patterns, in the kinds of things people expect, or fear, in the ways their ambitions are moulded, in their escape fantasies, and in their reaching out to the future. The business of making a religion for community-man must take account of every corner of human life. It must realize how men are affected by cultural changes, in the most practical details of economics and law. It must notice how people are changed politically, sexually and aesthetically.

This business of making a religion (though they wouldn't call it that) is employing the energies of writers and poets and politicians and economists and educationists and social workers and so on. Only a few of them are Christians, and those who are often do not see their Christianity as something that makes any special contribution to their work, beyond what is required by the nature of the job. But Christianity, for them, ought to throw a clearer light on the nature of the work to be done, and give it an assurance and a validity greater than can be assured by the natural hopefulness of human beings. Because of this it was delightful for Christians, concerned for the process of urgently needed cultural transition, to find that a comprehensive and persuasive version of a religion for community-man had already been worked out by Marxism. The excitement of this discovery was so great that some of the converts to the new religion were and remain gloriously blind to the failure of their religion to produce the results it ought to produce, just as some Catholic converts used to leap to enthusiastic defence of the Spanish Inquisition and the cult of St. Philomena. Both their compulsive blindness and the dismissive reactions to it are seen to be misplaced, once the nature of Marxism is recognized as religious. In other words, it is a cultural language, providing doctrine and morality and mythology in order to show the true destiny of man, and to evaluate the given cultural situation in the light of this destiny. As such it does not stand or fall by the degree of human goodness achieved by those whose culture it provides. It is, in any case, a new religion, and as such it doesn't function in a pure form but is modified by surviving layers of earlier cultures that now become a sort of spiritual underground, as paganism survived into the Christian culture in the form of witchcraft and folk-customs, as well as in less defined influences. But even when it has been apparently fully assimilated as a culture it cannot be judged except as a religion, and the standard of judgement here is not first of all whether it makes more people morally better according to some external standard, but whether it manages to articulate the needs and hopes and relationships of people involved in a particular kind of geographical and economic situation, in such a way as to make them able to cope with their lives and work towards the destiny which has been pointed out to them.

I am not attempting to make such a judgement here. I am not competent to do so and it is beside the point. The point is that Marxism is a religious phenomenon, and must be considered as such if its contribution to our understanding of human community is to be appreciated. If it is judged inadequate it can only be because it fails as a full articulation of those human needs and hopes that have been forced to the surface of living by the historical changes that I mentioned. And making this kind of judgement and acting on it is something that Christians should be concerned to do. For the Christian task in the understanding and creation of community is something much more than simply assisting the formation of a cultural awareness in the new situation. The Christian is bound to be active in encouraging and exploiting the most relevant and potentially fruitful cultural forms, and in noticing and fighting those aberrations of religious sense that always occur when a new culture is in process of formation. There are plenty at the moment. All this is commonplace in recent studies of the Christian's role in the modern world, and I think it is useful as far as it goes, but it does not go far enough. At a certain point it cannot give very convincing reasons for supposing that the Christian contribution is unique, or vital, and some writers have concluded that indeed it is not, and that Christianity as such must gradually fade out, having done its work of preparation for some new religion. Others continue to maintain that the Christian message is essential to the truly human development of man in the future, but the arguments put forward in support are sometimes more ingenious than powerful.

The reason for these patches of vagueness, covered over by a web of verbiage, seems to be that no-one is quite sure what exactly a truly human community is, and how it happens, therefore how you judge the spiritual quality of existing or emerging forms of community. In other words, the Christian religious language is not working properly as a means of evaluation. For instance, Harvey Cox suggests that secular man is pragmatic, and interested only in tackling specific problems. He also notices that urban culture produces an emotional "immunization" against close personal contacts other than those voluntarily chosen. He is careful to warn against certain aberrations of pragmatism, and is anxious that what he calls the new freedom to choose one's intimates should be used in a Christian way. But in both cases he accepts the qualities he describes as given, and justifies them elaborately with some rather selective exegesis. He has to, because the only way he can make sense of Christianity in the secular city is by assuming that the secular city is, though admittedly imperfectly, a manifestation of the Kingdom which is in process of realizing itself. This basic doctrine makes it possible for him to accept various aspects of life in the secular city as given, and he sees no need to judge them by any standards other than those of the secular city itself, validated as it is for him by scripture. He never asks whether secular pragmatism is a good thing, or whether the protective immunization against haphazard contacts is a convincing manifestation of the Kingdom. It is not possible to ask such questions unless one has the means to answer them, and that means some exterior standard of judgement: I am not saying that the secular city is *not* a manifestation of the Kingdom, or that such of its characteristics—if they are characteristic—as pragmatism and immunity to accidental relationships are evil. I am simply saying that in Dr. Cox's *The Secular City*, and in others in the same genre, no criteria are provided whereby such

41

things may be judged. This absence of criteria both leads, and in a curious way is due, to the acceptance as given of one contemporary form of association of human lives as an authentic though imperfect manifestation of the Kingdom in the modern world. Secular urbanism is being proposed as the new religious form of human life and it is proposed as therefore virtually self-validating. Religion and culture have become *identified*, and in this it is similar to other religious systems, including the medieval Catholic one. Lacking any external criteria for judging itself, the creation of this new religious culture is likely to fall into all the mistakes of the older ones, and the Christian who sees the task of Christianity as simply a scripturally enlightened and purposeful development as a religious culture of the given form of community-man is heading for yet another cultural, and religious, dead end.

In that case, where are we to find the criteria by which to judge the values and forms of the emerging culture? How are we to make Christianity *religious*? To judge the new cultural forms simply by the norms of earlier culture would be misguided, for that culture itself is subject to theological judgement. In fact many of the mistakes made by Christianity as a culture (or several cultures—one of the richest being the Orthodox) and from which we are having such difficulty in extricating ourselves, are due to a failure to judge these cultures by any criteria but their own internal ones. They failed, in fact, to be properly religious, in the sense of directing and evaluating the cultural situation according to relevant *theological* criteria.

I think we can get a bit nearer to discovering the kind of theological judgement that must be made, and how it works, if we take a look at the basic categories that St. Paul uses in his comments on aspects of community life, and see how they correspond to the actual experience of people engaged in living together. This should provide the basis for a real religious language for the culture of community, because it articulates a critique which relates the situation to something beyond itself, indeed beyond the religion which it requires in order to understand itself in terms of its ultimate meaning.

I think the first thing to emphasize, though it may seem too obvious to be worth mentioning, is that St. Paul is talking about real situations. The first letter to the Corinthians is a good example, for obvious reasons. Paul expects his readers to recognize at once the truth of what he is saying, when he points it out, although they had become so far blind to it that it needed pointing out. They had to have it pointed out precisely on account of the emotional situation on which he was commenting in chapter 3. Their rivalries and feuds were fogging their perceptions, they were wholly involved in a set of emotions that were what St. Paul calls "carnal" (or "natural", or "purely human" according to the theological bias of the translator). As long as the Corinthian community thought in categories of human allegiance and rivalry they were thinking as "worldly", "unspiritual" men, and were simply not able to make any other kind of judgement. But they were not wholly "unspiritual", they were at least "babes in Christ" and could therefore be expected to recognize in Paul's words a reminder of something they knew, but had allowed themselves to forget. He was recalling them to a different kind of awareness of living. "This is the Spirit we have received from God," he says, "and not the spirit of the world, so that we may know all that God of his grace gives us."

What they would recall at his reminder was something perfectly real, then, an experience of living sufficiently clear-cut to be referred to in the confidence that the reference would be immediately understood in the same way by all who heard it.

This experience of living was an experience of community, it was not just an individual experience of reconciliation. St. Paul refers to the congregation as a "building", and he is not referring to its *ad hoc* sociological shape—the simple fact of there being a number of like-minded people drawn together by their common ideals and having, necessarily, some sort of constitutional form. The bit about this is very interesting, verses 10–17:

"By the grace God gave me, I succeeded as an architect and laid the foundations on which someone else is doing the building. Everyone doing the building must work carefully. For the foundation, nobody can lay any other than the one which has already been laid, that is Jesus Christ. On this foundation you can build in gold, silver and jewels, or in wood, grass and straw, but whatever the material, the work of each builder is going to be clearly revealed when the day comes. That day will begin with fire, and the fire will test the quality of each man's work. If his structure stands up to it, he will get his wages. If it is burnt down, he will be the loser; and though he is saved himself, it will be as one who has gone through fire. Didn't you realize that you were God's Temple and that the Spirit of God was living among you? If anybody should destroy the Temple of God, God will destroy him, because the Temple of God is sacred; and you are that Temple."

It seems clear that St. Paul is talking about the making of the community as spiritual, whose foundation is Jesus Christ. And the "spiritual men" of this community are in a position to judge others, and this means not just to judge the individual, but also "the powers that rule the world", the whole set-up of the world, including its wise men, its orators, its scholars. The men of the community of the Spirit are not only *able* to judge the world, they are *bound* to do so, and this judgement of theirs is part of the process of overturning the old order. So there are two communities, and they are quite distinct and indeed incompatible with each other, but they are not sociologically separate, necessarily. This is apparent in two ways.

One is the reason for the letter—the fact that this community of people called to be men of the Spirit, has been behaving like "carnal" men. Its values have been those of a worldly community, it has been operating by the kinds of fears and jealousies and protective devices that are normal in a human community, large or small. Yet these people *are* Christians, they *are* "God's building".

The other way that this shows is in the description of the types of building that may be erected on the "foundation of Jesus Christ". It may be done with gold, silver and fine stone, or with wood, hay and straw. The building, then, is a human work and may be very variable in quality. The strength of the building depends on the abilities of the builder, but also on the quality of materials available. This shows how a religion is the language of a community in the Spirit—but this language and this community are "worldly" realities, created out of the given cultural situation. And so St. Paul recognizes that some building may not stand up to the final test, even though it is built on the foundation of Jesus Christ.

The interesting thing about this passage is that St. Paul makes it clear that there is some standard by which the quality of the building may be judged, and yet the building concerned is the Christian community, founded on Jesus Christ. It is quite specifically and unambiguously a Christian community, whose task is the overthrow of the existing order, yet the quality of the community life, the *religion* of the community, is still not necessarily good. St. Paul also says very unflattering things about the origins and abilities of his converts, as individuals, yet he has no hesitation in saying that "everything belongs to you—Paul, Apollos, and Cephas, the world, life and death, the present and the future". But this is because "you belong to Christ, and the Christ to God".

This is the standard by which the world is judged—"we possess the mind of Christ". This judgement is to be passed by the community of Christ on the community of the world, but this means that the Christian community is also judging itself, assessing its own quality. In that case the Christian community (a religious community) is worldly, that is, under judgement: it must be so, for a spiritual man is *not* "himself subject to judgement by his fellow men" yet there is no doubt that St. Paul judges the community, and expects its own conscience, as spiritual, to corroborate his judgement on it, that it is carnal and worldly.

All this is fairly obvious. It makes clear the fact that the Christian community is something other than the worldly community, in that it is charged with the religious task of judging the world, but that the Christian community itself is a worldly one, and under judgement as such. But it is not yet clear in what way this task of judging is one that belongs to the community. My thesis is that the Christian assembly not only has this task of judgement laid upon it, but that it is this act of judging which constitutes it as a community. Judgement is the heart of the theology of community, and this theology shows that in fact community as a fully authentic experience is a spiritual one, and therefore cannot be created by sociological expertise, though a proper setting is necessary if it is to flourish.

I think it may be shown that the task of judging the world is in fact the thing that makes the Christian group a community of the spirit. And as a corollary to this, the creation of a community of the Spirit is itself the act of judgement on the world, and this act of judgement is what "overthrows the existing order". This act of judgement by the community is a judgement of *itself*, and therefore overthrows itself, as worldly. But— and it is a big "but"—the community is, itself, an "existing order" and must continue to be so, to the end. It is a "building" which, as St. Paul says, may be made of any inadequate materials, but a building there must be. A religion is God's Temple—it is not God. It may be destroyed in the day of judgement, if its material is not of the kind that builds the true Kingdom, but that is God's act. The *man* who destroys the Temple is destroying himself, because he will then have no building, no community, no religion, in which and by which to exercise judgement.

The most effective way to show how this works is to make

use of examples. My first community is an imaginary one, but its truth to nature can unfortunately be verified without any difficulty at all. I have made up this one only to avoid singling out any particular real one. This first one is a family, which is a common and basic kind of community and can also be in every way a community in the spirit in the sense in which St. Paul describes it. The reason why I have chosen a family as an example of a "worldly" community is in order to show how easily the outward form of community can be emptied of the spirit and become merely a defensive alliance, or a mutual benefit society. My imaginary family is not especially "typical", but it is not at all uncommon. Some of the reasons why it has failed to be a community in the spirit are evident in circumstances, while others have deeper cultural roots.

This family has a widowed mother, whose husband was a local government official. He died when the eldest son was in his middle teens, and this son is now grown up and works in the local library. Two other children are still at school, one girl is at college. The family's income is very restricted, and it is always difficult to make ends meet. They live, therefore, on the fringe of a respectable district of an industrial town, where it shades off into the less desirable parts. The mother, though not especially well educated herself, is proud of her intelligent children and determined to give them the kind of standards she had as a girl (in the days when money bought more) in a doctor's family with a comfortable income, servants and a large garden. Her husband was clever but slightly embittered by early poverty, and from him she gets her determination that the children shall be cultured and well educated as well as well mannered, well dressed and respectable. The eldest son, introduced to the responsibility of a sort of fatherhood at a sensitive age, is broodily and intolerantly determined on the same things, and is much more censorious about any lapses than his mother. So the younger children are strictly brought up, they go to expensive private schools even at the cost of no

47

holidays and endless fuss about turning lights off and eating margarine. To compensate for the financial hardships the whole family cultivate an intense tribal pride in their special traditions, and in their cultural superiority to other families they know. It is this that keeps them going, and makes them a very closely knit and loyal family. They are proud of each other and devoted to each other. The shifts and moral evasions that are forced on them by the need to maintain their unity and morale are not acknowledged. They cannot be, because the very existence of the family as a family depends on its members never questioning the worth-whileness of all that they do in order to preserve the kind of life they have created. In preserving the tradition they show courage, patience, diligence and thoughtfulness for each other's welfare even at the expense of personal comfort and profit. The reverse side of this is necessarily a deep intolerance of other families living nearby who are less well educated, or less well behaved, though possibly better off financially. They have a lack of compassion for people who fail in any undertaking, and this rules out entirely any contact with the poor or socially deprived. This even includes members of the family. Failure to achieve the family's goals is *the* sin, because it undermines their confidence in the absolute worth-whileness of their efforts and sufferings. Such failure, and the ever-present fear of it, leads to quarrels and bitter reproaches and rivalries, to partisanship and to a refusal of real intimacy even to each other, in case hidden weakness should be unmasked. Yet this is a community, and a very effective one.

There are many admirable things about a community like this. It has the kind of tenacity that maintains a backbone of determination to survive in times of social upheaval, and makes it possible for a later generation to re-discover the values of a past age and make use of them. It is the sort of thing the monasteries of Europe did at one time. But such a community can only do this by rejecting all change as necessarily evil. Its religion—its notion of its own meaning and purpose as a community—is identified with its given cultural situation, therefore to change the cultural set-up would be to abandon the religion. It cannot afford to recognize any standard of judgement outside itself. It corresponds very closely to St. Paul's description of the carnal, worldly community, both in its admirable and in its unpleasant aspects. It displays wisdom, strength, order, observance of law. It rejects as the ultimate destructive folly any admission of weakness or ignorance. It "refuses what belongs to the Spirit of God", as St. Paul puts it, because this Spirit judges it, and tests it, by a standard other than that of its own goals. In order to maintain this refusal and protect its own necessary self-confidence, it must refuse admittance, communally and individually, to any influences that would undermine the barriers between people. Each must keep *to* himself, and when their isolation is threatened each reacts with anger and malice. For instance, St. Paul says he tries to meet everyone half-way in order not to upset well-meaning people or offend the consciences of others: no member of this all-too-imaginable family is capable of that because to do so would be to admit that there might be other standards of judgement than those imposed by the community's own aims and structure.

It would be extremely difficult to alter a community formed in such a way. It is easier to realize this in the case of a small family community, where the emotional set-up can be examined in detail, and this is why I chose it. It is easy to see how very drastic an event would be required to alter such a pattern of living and thinking. If it *were* altered by, say, one of the daughters having an illegitimate child, or the mother marrying again, the chances are that the family, as a community, would simply break up. Such an event would demand responses of a kind that are incompatible with the forces that hold the community in being. This demand would, in fact, constitute a kind of judgement, which could not be accepted. The "unspiritual man" cannot grasp it, as St. Paul says. It

49

must be ignored, if possible, and if it is not possible the community simply disintegrates, as such, though its members may continue to live together out of force of habit, and for lack of any other pattern of living. But the sense of confidence and purpose that bound the members together will be absent, and the situation can only deteriorate, unless there is some drastic intervention of a kind that breaks through to the surviving "spiritual" reality and re-makes the family, or part of it, as a community in the spirit.

It is unnecessary to underline the points of similarity between the situation of this miniature community and that of the historical Catholic Church in certain aspects. The resemblance is sufficiently obvious, and the emotional forces that create and maintain and also threaten such a community will be found to be the same in both cases. Other Churches and sects have shown similar symptoms.

This kind of community cannot accept judgement. We need to know what kind of community *can* accept judgement, and be re-made by it. The example I have chosen for this is a real one, and a well-known one, but it is happily not at all unusual, and could be paralleled in any age or place where people allow the Spirit to work and to change their lives in his own way.

I would emphasize that although this community owed its existence to the spiritual clear-sightedness of one man, Abbé Henri Pierre, he could have done nothing unless he had been going with the tide of the Spirit, which moves people in certain definite ways, and works according to definite principles and conditions, whether or not the people concerned realize it. It was unplanned, it simply occurred, one thing leading to another because people responded to situations in a certain way.

In 1950 Abbé Pierre was a member of the French *Chambre des Députés*, so he looked for somewhere cheap to live and work in or near Paris. He heard of a house in the suburbs that was going cheap because although it was big it was in a near-ruined condition and had no heating or electricity. But the fabric was sound, so he took it and set about doing repairs and renovations in his spare time. Because it was obviously too big for one man, he offered it to youth groups and organizations for gatherings, for study groups and conferences or retreats. It proved a great success, and as some people wanted to stay whole weekends he bought camp beds and equipped the place as a rough-and-ready hostel. It was at this stage that he called the place "Emmaus", because it was a home outside the capital city where people came who were looking for God.

One day someone told the Abbé that an ex-convict not far away had tried to commit suicide because the family situation he came home to was so appalling that he couldn't face it. Instead of trying to console the man in a situation which offered no hope, the Abbé said, "I need someone to come and give me a hand. Come with me and we can work together." The man came and lived at "Emmaus", did odd jobs, shared the life. A few others turned up, or were brought—drop-outs, ex-prisoners, a man from the Foreign Legion. They were people whom society had totally rejected, who were hopeless and embittered. They stayed and helped, some left, and came back again. They were a sort of family. When the Abbé lost his seat as a Député, and therefore his salary on which the "family" had existed, it was one of these men who suggested that rag-picking—scrounging in dustbins and refuse heaps for saleable rubbish, or house-to-house collecting of stuff from people's cellars and attics—could provide an income to keep the place going. But just before this "Emmaus" had taken in not only a few down-and-outs, and the visiting organizations, but an evicted family who had happened to hear that there might be room at "Emmaus". It was through taking in this family that what came to be called the "Society of Rag-pickers" became aware of the appalling housing conditions of hundreds of families crowded in leaky basements, of others still worse off in sheds, tents, or holes, of children dying and men and women going mad. And because the government departments would do nothing, the rag-pickers did something. It happened because they had been putting up dormitories and halls for the youth groups, at "Emmaus", from ex-army huts, and they had some materials left over. Why not build a little house for this family which has come here, they said. So they built it—quite legally —on a poor bit of land the Abbé had bought with his Député's salary. The family moved in but, the Abbé said later "there was still some ground left, and some materials lying around, and also in the meantime more families had come along and told us what a desperate condition they were in. Well, we were so carried away by enthusiasm at all this that we used up everything that was left and the result was a house nearly seventy feet long. It had fifteen rooms in it, and five families. All done in four months! . . . It had only been possible because all the materials were on the spot, and all the work had been done free of charge by the community and by young helpers . . . by Christmas the five families were in."

The story of their achievement in promoting cheap housing, and even procuring changes in the law, made headlines. The dogged, usually illegal, and genially defiant programme of actually building small but decent houses brought it about. So did the outcry that occurred when a baby died of cold in an old caravan where his parents—with dozens of others—were living in a makeshift encampment while they waited for the Rag-pickers to finish their houses. The demand naturally exceeded their ability to meet it quickly. The Abbé told the nation about it, on the radio, and the results followed which brought hope to thousands of desperate people. But none of this would have happened if there had not been a little nucleus of men, the "Community of Emmaus", who made their living and brought hope to the poorest, by working on the rubbish dumps, and who found themselves as human beings by doing so. St. Paul would have recognized what the Abbé meant by the "en-thusiasm" that "carried away" the community of Rag-pickers. He would have described them as "on fire with the Spirit".

But this is interesting—the community did not come first, and then set about helping the needy—it became a community in the Spirit in response to the demand made on its members when they realized that they, the off-scourings of society in St. Paul's phrase, had something to give to people in still greater misery. Though their motives in coming to "Emmaus" may originally have been merely need for shelter, or the hope of scrounging an easy living off the mad priest, they did not remain together out of fear, or self-interest. They were held together as a community by this unexpected demand, which generated between them a bond of respect and affection and responsibility—a bond of love, in fact, though probably they would not have called it that.

But there is more to it than that. The fact of what they were, as well as what they did, constituted a challenge. It was a judgement on an apathetic society that did not want to think about the misery of homelessness and desperate poverty. The Rag-pickers scooped up society's sins and flicked the filth in its collective face, not deliberately, but simply by being what they were and doing—quite quietly—what they did.

Abbé Pierre described very well this double action of the Spirit, which draws people together in a community of the Spirit, and by so doing passes judgement on the world. He was talking later to people who had not utterly lost all hope, and with it the will to act, but, as he said, "felt hounded and crushed by the mechanisms of the societies to which they belong". And this is his advice: "Learn to unite and to turn your eyes, and the strength you gain from uniting, not first of all towards the people above you, but towards those who are less fortunate than yourselves. And putting this strength at the service of your less fortunate brethren, save yourselves and others too, and by saving others, the most desperate ones of all, you will hurl a stone of scandal in amongst the fortunate ones."

This is what a community in the Spirit does, and the fact of

53

doing it defines its own self-consciousness. This particular example came into being in the service of the most desperate of all, but of course this is not the only motivation. Abbé Pierre himself compared the movement to the one that arose round St. Benedict, and described the Rag-pickers, significantly, as the "new monks". What makes a community in the Spirit is not its particular work, but the fact that it is composed of people who are not afraid to love and to give because they are humble—that is, they know that they are judged and are not destroyed by this, but find peace in it, and hope. By doing so they are themselves a judgement on the world. This is why such communities have always aroused fierce anger and hatred, as the Abbé was denounced as a communist, and an agitator greedy for power, and his friends as a subversive force, undermining law and order and spreading anarchy.

There was, and there always is, some superficial excuse for such complaints, because—as in the days of Jesus himself—it is the poor who listen most readily to the spirit. These poor are the financially badly off, but also especially the poor in spirit, the sinners, the drop-outs and rejects, the oddities who don't fit in. They have nothing to lose, having lost so much already of the things by which respectable people reckon human value.

Like the earliest Christian gatherings, this particular Temple of God, this odd little human community that gathered round the eccentric Abbé, was not built of very good materials. It was built as all human communities are, of the materials available, and in this case they were weakened by bad education, poor heredity, the effects on children and adolescents of early insecurity and fear, as well as of adult misfortune and crime. But there is no doubt that it was a Temple of God, and anyone who tried to destroy such a building, however good his intentions according to the values of the world, was and is destroying the spirit in himself. For the very existence of a community of this kind is not only evidence that it has accepted judgement and been formed by it, but is itself a judgement on all who come in contact with it. Just by being there it judged, it exposed, it divided. So there were people who would have liked to destroy it, to put the Rag-pickers in prisons, mental homes, homes for the aged, who wanted to split up the homeless families and put the children in orphanages, to wipe out the whole affair, because it didn't fit the world's standards of success. By going on being there, in its muddly way, it accused them, "for God chose what is weak in the world to shame the strong".

The thing that made this odd "family" a community in the Spirit was the acceptance of judgement. It knew itself judged as unspiritual, and was able to accept that judgement because it was also, already, spiritual and able to hear, being poor in spirit. It did not reject the judgement as a better equipped community might have done, because it was not a community that was strong in the wisdom of the world.

Oddly enough, it is by being willing to be judged as worldly that a community can re-make itself as spiritual, therefore not depending for its existence on worldly achievement (necessary though that may be at the minimum level of practical organization). And as spiritual it is *not* subject to judgement, but on the contrary, judges others.

I think there is a clue in this experience to the double rôle of the Christian community, of which only one part is recognized in some current versions.

That one part is, as I suggested earlier, the important task of observing and guiding the emergence of a valid culture for the time. It has to provide a specific religious language that can articulate the purposes and assumptions of the culture and give them direction. If religion is language about the purpose and destiny of man, a bad or one-sided religion can and does distort a culture and eventually destroy people. But this religion-making is a human, worldly task, it is the building of the Temple, as skilfully as possible, with the available materials. Yet if this building is to be the Temple of God, whatever its materials, and not simply the Town Hall, the building must be undertaken by people who know that their work (that is, their community and its religion) is under judgement. They must know that the wisdom of the world is insufficient though necessary. It is only by this acceptance of the transience of their work, and in fact its essential worldliness, that the community of the Spirit can be created. The Church itself can only be the community of the Spirit by knowing that it is the community of the world, and continuing to work, as worldly, under judgement. The judgement it undergoes makes it spiritual and makes it able to judge the world, including itself. It makes it capable of creating a religious form that truly speaks about the cultural situation, but also evaluates it and guides it towards a hope beyond any particular culture.

This Christian community, then, which is and has to be worldly, knows itself under judgement, is therefore repentant, and reconciled. The scruffy group of drop-outs who formed the first "Emmaus Community" would not have recognized themselves in such a description, but it is theologically accurate. And by being this community, created by judgement, it is itself a judgement. This is the unique task of the Christian community, by which and *only* by which it can have the special discernment that enables it to help in its other related task of making a religious language.

Its unique task might be described as that of breaking vicious circles. I described such a vicious circle in the case of my first family, whose pride was based on their high cultural standards, who maintained those standards by never admitting that they could fail, and who prevented that failure by cultivating an intense pride, and so on. The existence of a community such as my second example would constitute a judgement of their way of life, and if that judgement were accepted it would break the circle. I suggested this would be unlikely to happen, but if once it were admitted that the love that made this second community was a value more important than achievement or self-defence then that would be a judgement, it would have

THE EXPERIENCE OF COMMUNITY

broken the circle. The kind of small weak group represented by the "Emmaus Community" is capable of doing just that. This is the reason why politically powerless communities have sometimes appeared to powerful governments as a threat to be ruthlessly crushed. A State that keeps its power by a circle of propaganda and publicized achievement, leading to more propaganda and requiring yet more achievement, is always vulnerable to the existence of a community, or even an individual, openly operating by values other than those of the State's own hopes and fears. This is one reason for the persecution of the early Christians, of some medieval sects, of the Puritans in Elizabethan England, and of Quakers in New England. Such a group is a judgement on the larger society, simply by existing. The judgement must be accepted, and the larger community thereby radically changed, or else the source of the challenge must be ruthlessly suppressed.

Here we come up against a difficulty which is always present. As soon as such a community, large or small, tries to bring its own powers of judgement to bear on the situation by unspiritual means it is no longer acting as the power of God's judgement. It may be obliged to do this as part of its task of religion-making, but if it does so it must do it in the knowledge that this is a worldly task, according to the wisdom of the world, and is therefore under judgement. I am not saying it should not be done, I am simply pointing out what seems to me to be the theological status of what is done. It is *not* the act of God's judgement, the one which creates the community as spiritual, and so makes it a judgement on the world. It is only a bit of human building, valuable as that may be. And it must therefore recognize itself as under judgement. As soon as it regards this worldly task as a *spiritual activity*, and so one *not* subject to judgement, it is guilty of blasphemy, it is rejecting God's judgement and is itself condemned. In that case it is no longer able to be the power of God to overturn the existing order, what Paul calls the "things that are". On the contrary it must itself be overturned. Which seems to be in part what is happening to the Church at present.

To sum up, I am suggesting that the study of actual experience as a source of the theology of community shows that the Christian community has two tasks, which are not separable but are distinct. And these two tasks are what make it a community—a wordly community, and *also* a community of the Spirit; that is, the Temple of God. The community has to organize itself, and organize with others, in order to bring to bear on its own worldly situation the understanding it gains in its calling. This is its task of religion-making. But in order to do this truly, and make a religion which can worship God and not idols, it must also come into being as a community made, not by hands, but by the act of God. This act is an act of judgement, and it is by undergoing this judgement that the community exists as spiritual. By this also it is enabled both to *be* and to *utter* God's judgement on the world, which includes its own worldly building. And in this capacity, again in relation to its *own* organization as well as to other worldly organisms, it has a unique power to break the circles of pride and fear and hate. *Only* the Spirit can do this, when he acts in people and sets them free to love each other, for it is love which is the naked power of the Spirit that breaks down barriers and sets people free.

Important and essential as the work of Temple building may be, it seems to me that this other, complementary task is more important, especially at this time. We are in some danger of overlooking it, through the re-discovered emphasis on the worldly task of Christians. But the worldly task can easily become simply a matter of rearranging people's fears and prejudices in a way that fits more conveniently into the pattern of modern life, as in the example I gave of the emotional immunity to casual human contacts that city-dwellers develop. If we are to avoid this danger, and also clearly to preach the Gospel, we have to keep on remembering what it is that makes us a community in the Spirit and gives us any claim to have a rôle in the world at all. And that is our awareness of judgement. Breaking the vicious circle is something no-one else can do because no-one else sees that it needs doing. Most people assume that you just make the circle wider, or stronger, or more flexible. But we have to *break* it. We can think of the circle of hate and fear and cruelty in race relations, of the circle of insecurity and rapaciousness and competitiveness in a capitalist economy, of the circle of fear and jealousy and suspicion and ruthlessness in international affairs. It is not hard to think of many more.

I am not proposing solutions, or delineating tidily the Christian task in these messy situations. I only want to suggest that what makes a community in the Spirit is the same thing that makes it able to be the act of God in history, making that history towards its end. I am saying that, since it is primarily God who acts, we should be careful of telling God what he ought to do, or rather of assuming that what seems sensible to us must be the power of the Spirit at work—whether it be in a Vatican form or a New Left form. And I am concluding that the Christian community is uniquely itself, and uniquely the act of God, when, knowing itself under judgement, it becomes thereby the judgement of God on this generation.

When it is fully itself the Christian community, not only under judgement but knowing it, and knowing what that means, is in the best possible position to develop the religious implications of the philosophy of man as a community creature. But the main task of the Christian community is simply to let itself be formed by, and so to become, the judgement of God.

3. The Experience of Ministry

THE experience of actual communities helps to open up approaches to a theology of community, and I suggested in the last chapter that this study of actual experience tells us quite a lot about what kind of community the Church is, ought to be, or fails to be—and why. It seems useful, therefore, to take a closer look at one aspect of life as the Church is actually living through it now, and see what the experience of ministry in the community is like. One thing this shows us, eventually, is that this is not a separate problem, but that the experience of ministry does not so much throw light on a theology of ministry as illuminate our notion of what the whole Christian community is like.

As a problem, the status of the ministry is an acute practical one in all the churches. It takes a particular form in the Catholic Church of which I am a member, because of its tradition of celibacy and of a special clerical mystique and the prestige that goes with it. But the experience of contemporary Catholic ministry is only one especially agonizing example of the need which has become urgent in all the churches, to reexamine the whole meaning of the ministry, in a time of radical change. The place to start that re-examination is by reflection on actual experience, which is different in different times and places, but which can help to elucidate basic principles when it is properly understood. We cannot lay down a theological basis divorced from particulars, and then apply them to all times and places—this method has been tried all too often, with disastrous results. (The fate of Matteo Ricci's mission to China is only one glaring example.) We must try to understand the theology

60

by seeing how the Spirit actually works in people who try to obey his promptings. Then, carefully and respectfully, we can use this understanding to help in directing and developing the particular case.

At the moment, argument in all the churches on issues with a theological basis is frequently motivated by fears and prejudices rather than by study of the facts of actual experience. In times of crisis such as the present, Christians always have been inclined to get very worked up about the theological issues, and in a sense it is right that they should. Acrimony is better than apathy. But it is helpful to our understanding of the kind of crisis in which we are involved to see which particular issues are the ones that excite people just now. The excitement is, naturally, only articulated by a comparatively small number of people—hence the complaints in all the churches about a "vocal minority" who do not represent the general view. But even if the more extreme views are minority ones the actual subjects for debate are ones which cause concern even to those who find it difficult to say what they are worried about, or what should be done about it. So the minority are vocal and the mass silent but worried about such varied subjects as the role of the minister (and whether he should be celibate), the style of worship and the place of the laity in the actual running of the Church. Among Catholics leading subjects are the power of the Pope and its possible limitations, the method of choosing bishops, the place of women and the importance of religious life. A list for Anglicans would include the question of disestablishment, which of the new forms of Communion Service is bearable, as well as worries they share with Catholics, or with other Christians. Methodists debate the value of the circuit as opposed to the settled Minister, and so on.

Such lists are familiar and we may be inclined to take them for granted, but it is useful to take a second look, because they aren't, after all, as obvious as it seems at first sight. These are all important subjects, certainly, but there are others, which

61

might be debated with equal heat, and which indeed have been debated in the past. We might, for instance, be concerned with clashes over the human nature of Christ, the worth of penitential practices, the fate of the unbaptized, the relationship between Father, Son and Spirit, the relative value of formal public worship and *extempore* prayer, the morality of usury or military service, the Second Coming—and so on. All of these are, in fact, debated even now, but generally only among groups who happen to be interested or affected by them, and care enough to argue. But the first list of issues is of subjects on which virtually all Christians who think at all about their religion (even if it is only a casual argument over a pint) have opinions one way or the other. The other topics, much more diverse and in some cases more fundamental to our faith, would leave most ordinary churchgoers bewildered, uninterested, and without any clear opinion to offer.

Why do ordinary Christians feel more interest in the nature of the ministry than in the nature of Christ? Why does the language or style of public liturgy rouse more feeling than the value of private inspiration? Why is the power of the Pope a more explosive topic for Catholics and Protestants alike than the procession of the Spirit? A quick answer might be, because the former are closer to us, more manageable subjects. But this is not good enough, when we remember that people once came to blows over the theology of the Incarnation, and that whole new churches came into being on the basis of a high valuation for private inspiration. I think there is a more powerful reason than these, and it may be discerned by asking what the various contentious subjects in my first list have in common.

What they have in common is that they are all concerned with rôle and identity. Even the liturgy arguments can be seen to derive their energy from the fact that the liturgy, better than anything else, defines and expounds what is the nature of the community that worships. All the churches have had equally acrimonious debates on these subjects, for the same reasons.

Are Catholics building "a bridge to Protestantism"? Are Anglicans giving in to Rome? What is a Catholic anyway? What is a Protestant? What is a priest? Is he different from a parson or minister? What is the Pope? What, finally, is the Church and who belongs to it? And these are not academic questions, or matters we need to understand clearly, simply in order to enlighten inquirers. It isn't even a question of deepening our faith and understanding in order to be truer to the Church and Christ's will for it. It is a matter of sheer survival.

It has become embarrassingly clichéed to talk about an "identity crisis", and many people who use the phrase don't really know what they are talking about. It often sounds as if it were a matter of fearing to lose one's prestige or self-respect. It can entail both of these, but what is hitting Christians of all shades is the fear of a loss of self. That is why they get less worked up about inspiration or the Blessed Trinity, and more about whether the priest is a sacrificing creature and whether a Catholic is really anything but a Protestant who hasn't yet shifted the Pope. You can't worry too much about the nature of the God who calls you to be his son if you aren't sure whether you stand in the kind of relation to God that could make sense of son-ship, and how, if at all, such a relation can be made explicit in the community: if indeed a community can be said to exist in this context, as opposed to that of the brotherhood of man alone.

This problem is very well recognized, and all kinds of people are hard at work offering solutions in books, sermons and movements. Whether the cure is seen as a return to the traditional Catholic vision of the orderly, splendid Church which is supposed to have existed before the Council (it never did—the memories of polemicists are wonderfully short) or as the scrapping of everything since Constantine in favour of an evangelical vision of a charismatic association of little groups of zealous, undogmatic leftist saints (modelled on a notion of the early Church which never existed either), the desire generally seems to be to abolish uncertainty in favour of a clear, understandable state of affairs. It is assumed that the agonizing and bickering and doubts, the personal collapses and the groups' pugnacities, are things that should not happen. The reasons given for their happening vary according to one's point of view—for instance a priest is said to leave the ministry because he hadn't a sufficiently solid grounding in the spiritual life and couldn't stand up to the stress and temptation of the times; alternatively it is suggested that he left because the ministry as it exists at present came to seem anachronistic, a perpetuation of a system that should be abolished to make way for more relevant forms. The two explanations are not, in fact, contradictory. The stresses and temptations of the time do demand a very deep and powerful spirituality, and two of the temptations are to feel that the "system" is as fixed as it would like to be thought, and that a "relevant" ministry is going to emerge from the oven, all hot and ready, without any previous cookery.

It may help to untangle a little of the incidental complications of what has been called the "clerical neurosis" if I quote the cases of two typical men at present working in the Christian ministry, but tackling the same problem in very different ways. Their ideas and problems can occur in more than one denominational setting. In both of these the "clerical neurosis" is in fact mild, because they had a lot to do of an obviously useful kind, and they had other kinds of psychological support which are not always to be found, but their experience, which is quite common, throws light on the general problem.

A. is naturally rather conservative, deeply pious and acknowledged as holy, even by those who laugh at his devotions. He is not especially intelligent though anything but a fool, and by no means at ease with high-powered contemporary theology, though reasonably familiar with its more obvious aspects. B. is far more intelligent and dynamic, a natural leader and an enthusiast for reform, thoughtful and well read in theology and psychology, whole-heartedly behind the move to up-date the

64

Church, though slowed down by his situation and the views of people he has to work with; a good, prayerful man, though perhaps not sufficiently aware of some of his own motives. Both of these men are anxious to give the laity in their charge the chance to discover a genuine Christian life. A. tries to do this by encouraging people to work things out for themselves and try out solutions. He is worried and even shocked by some ideas that come up, and will argue and condemn, but he is prepared to trust people and give them a chance to prove themselves right. The result is that renewal of a fairly radical kind gets underway fast, not on a doctrinaire basis but because this seems to be what the particular situation demands, if people are to get the Christian message. He himself becomes unpopular with some other clergy, who feel that he is losing control and not doing his duty as a priest. He also suffers a good deal from self-doubt, and anxiety about the rightness of some of what is being done. The whole situation, also, is vulnerable, because it is working (very well) on an *ad hoc* basis and it must be difficult to discover a firm theoretical institutional basis which can survive if he, or his first collaborators, should move elsewhere.

B., to the astonishment of some, moves more slowly although his ideas are much more clearly and certainly radical. He believes firmly in letting the laity run things, but he tells them when to do it and how much. He prevents irresponsible and premature experiment and thus reduces the risk of failure, and the loss of confidence that follows. On the other hand, since he decides when and where to hand over responsibility, he doesn't allow much room for the emergence of lay leadership, or any leadership other than his own. This is not his intention, but it happens. He cannot generate as much enthusiasm as he had hoped, and is often disappointed. The ideas and initiative are his, and he knows they are good—both realistic and full of potential for the future—and he cannot see why they do not "catch" as he knows they should. But progress has been made, his leadership is sound and his personal influence excellent. He is respected, sometimes loved, and obeyed with understanding and goodwill, in most cases.

Here is an apparent paradox. The one with clear, radical ideas, lots of imagination and a strong belief in the importance of lay management and initiative produces, in practice, a fairly "traditional" type of set-up, from the psychological point of view. That is, he is the natural leader, the symbol of the Church, the guide and upholder, the person to turn to in difficulties and for reassurance in uncertainty and anxiety. On the other hand the naturally "traditional" clergyman, devout in the old way and uneasy with radical theology, produces a situation that would delight the upholder of a radical ecclesiology. Because of his love and respect for his people he gives them responsibility of a kind that does not depend on him, ultimately, but is really their own, to use or misuse. He is their comforter, adviser and friend, but not their leader, and some of them miss this in practice even while they applaud it in theory. But a few—very few—are growing in their Christian awareness through this experience, and discovering a new appreciation of the minister's role as one of spiritual focus and "pointer"—a sort of prophetic role, in fact, though the word has wildish overtones that are not true to this particular situation.

These two types, which can be found, with variations, in all denominations that have an ordained ministry, help to make clear a very subtle but important distinction. The priest or minister, in a community, if he is to be more than a sacramental power-point (even fitted with an adapter), must be this kind of prophetic thing, and also the link with the rest of the "institutional" Church. ("Institution" is a perfectly good word, for an essential thing, even if the actual one is often clumsy and distorted.) This is minimal, and has nothing to do with his personality. He is the sign of what the Church is about, whether he likes it or not, and if he is a bad one he causes scandal. Theologically, there seems to be no need to demand more; "all" he has to do is to try to live up to the measure of the sign he inevitably is—that is, to be Christlike.

So far so good. But the actual experience of the ministry seldom stops at that, because most Christians want a lot of things
from their minister that the theology of Christian ministry does
not at first sight strictly require. They want him to be not only
the *sign* of the Christian "thing" but also the *fact* of it. They
want him not only to signify the reality of the Spirit among
them, but to *be* the Spirit—guiding, enlightening, admonishing
and judging. Like B. in the case I described, some priests have
the kind of personality that can cope with this quite well, and
the results are often excellent. Others have fewer of the qualities
required but do take it for granted that this kind of thing is
part of their job. It "always has been" and if they were not
expected to provide this kind of leadership they would feel lost
and offended. It is this type (minister, clergyman or priest) that
is most worried by attempts to reassert the reductively theological, as opposed to the psychological, significance of the
Christian ministry. It makes him feel unimportant.

But there is another kind of worry, which afflicts neither of
the two men I described, because one was not obliged to exercise a psychological function he had successfully handed over,
and the other exercised the same function with ease and bril-
liance. This worry is, I think, at the root of the clerical neurosis
in its most common form. It is an increasing fear and dislike of
being made into the "thing" symbolized, as well as the symbol.
Some clergy complain that people expect them to embody the
laity's disillusion with the institution, their hopes and dreams
of a renewed Church, and of course to carry the can if there is
trouble. Others complain of the same tendency in another
form, for people who are bewildered and suspicious of changes
demand from the clergy a strong hand to support them through
their difficulties, a clear and simple exposition of what is right,
what is wrong and what is going to happen, and of course a
firm and instant assurance that all is well. Both of these kinds
of demand are, in spite of the difference in form, really the

same demand. Both require that the minister should be, personally, what his office symbolizes. And such demands, in either form, are acceptable and indeed necessary to some ministers. These may be the kind who love the exhilaration of leadership and struggle, whose sense of vocation and of personal value is dependent on being the object of such requirements. They may have the "old-fashioned" view which simply takes it for granted that this is part of the job, which is one they can cope with without strain. And "old-fashioned" in this sense, as I suggested, means their sense of rôle, not their theological views, which may be radical. (In this context, this means reductionist, in reaction to the inflated clerical image of the immediate past.)

But there are an increasing number, especially among the more sensitive and thoughtful clergy, who realize that this demand that they be what their office symbolizes can be, and often is, a distortion of the life of the community and an attempt on the part of other Christians to avoid responsibility. Some can see this and still cope because they are resilient and optimistic personalities and hope to alter the situation or at least carry it, while hoping for better things. Others, less hopeful, see this distortion as inherent in the present forms of the Church institutions, and see no likelihood of change from within. They know themselves to be, like other Christians, struggling through a period of change and experiment, groping for signs of the way ahead, and they don't feel able to be this kind of effective symbol that people want. It seems to them to be a kind of hypocrisy either to let themselves appear to be the standards of revolt and renewal, or to suggest, by continued membership of it, that the clerical institution of whatever denomination can provide the kind of ministry which the future Church requires.

The people who feel like this are not all young and not all "progressive" in their thinking. There are others, both young and old, whose thinking is traditional, but who, at a certain point, suddenly find that they are no longer supported by the old sense of the absolute value, regardless of personal failures, of the clerical role. One conventional and hard-working parish priest in late middle-age was heard to say, almost in tears, "they want so much, and I've got nothing to give them". Yet, twenty years ago, he would probably have been upheld by confidence in the time-honoured role of the priest, and would have been sure that this, in itself, would give his people something valuable, even if he personally were insignificant and weak. What would once have been a personal spiritual crisis of self-knowledge, very painful but recognizable in terms of traditional spirituality, has now become a crisis of rôle. It can take the form of "I *can't* be the kind of *person* people want a priest to be, perhaps I should leave the ministry", or "I *must not* be the kind of minister that people want me to be, because I am not that kind of person and anyway they want the wrong kind of ministry, so perhaps I should leave".

Some do leave and some don't. For Roman Catholic clergy the marriage question is often the deciding one, because if a woman turns up who seems to offer an alternative meaning and purpose in life of an obviously valuable kind, then the increasingly hollow role of the priest immediately looks even less possible and even less sensible and truthful. But this isn't always the case. There are some men who leave the ministry, although they have a clear and satisfactory sense of the priestly vocation and little doubt of their ability to fill the role reasonably well. They are not too much disturbed by what they recognize as the inevitable though un-ideal psychological demands of the people they serve. If a man of this kind leaves and gets married it may be because he has discovered that he can't cope with celibacy, or because one particular woman has insensibly become so necessary to him, and he to her, that the alternative to marriage seems to be intolerable personal disablement and distortion. Their judgement about this may or may not be a true one, but this is how things seem, and such a decision is not a rejection of the role of the Christian minister, except in so far as the present Catholic discipline makes it impossible to continue in it after marriage.

This kind of thing is not new at all; since clerical celibacy became the rule in the Western Church there have been men who decided that it was impossible for them personally, either negatively (because they felt they couldn't do without sex) or positively (because they discovered a profound need for one particular woman). Sometimes they left the ministry, sometimes they kept the woman as a mistress, and in the Middle Ages this last was so common as to be accepted as a normal thing even if it was not approved by the Church. At all times, if the man was a good priest and loved by his people, they forgave him, and tacitly accepted the situation, thinking little the worse of him. In the same way, before the days of acceptable divorce, Anglicans were tolerant of the marital indiscretions of their clergy if the individual man was loved and respected as a priest. This still goes on, but because of the more general undermining of clerical self-confidence it is becoming less and less common. More often, now, the man leaves the ministry.

Apart from this effect of increasing the number of men who leave the Catholic ministry and marry rather than stay in it and keep a mistress quietly, this older and indeed permanent problem of a celibate clergy is quite separate from the widespread clerical neurosis, which is new. It is a mistake to confuse the two, because it makes it difficult to see what is really the matter, and celibacy is not primarily what is the matter. The Anglican and other non-Catholic clergy are suffering in similar ways, and there is no celibacy problem for them. Celibacy does come into the picture in another way, however, in that it is the Catholic version of the ideal image of the Christian minister, and helps to create a kind of demand for a totally adequate personal embodiment of what the priest symbolizes by his office. To that extent the revulsion from celibacy reinforces for Catholics the general revulsion from a role that seems not only unattainable but wrong and hypocritical. It seems to bring the mystique of the priesthood too close to what the tempter offered Adam and Eve: you shall be as gods.

It seems possible, then, that the painfulness for many of the experience of ministry is due, basically, to a confusion in practice between the essential "significant" role of the presbyter (to use the archaic, and theologically neutral term), and his traditional but incidental practical role as leader, judge and "father". The virtually universal coincidence of the two in the past had led to a situation in which there is on the one hand a fear of complete loss of personal meaning if the "leader and father" aspect is eroded by the "new theology" and on the other to a restless desire that the "reductive" theological notion should be developed. There is also a corresponding dislike and even fear of the laity's continuing demand for the traditional image, which prevents any alternative unfolding of the presbyter's practical rôle.

In trying to clarify the workings of this "crisis of ministry" it may be helpful to make use of a very simple and ordinary parallel example which lies within the experience of everyone. This is the mother–child relationship, though here I have described what it can and should be, ignoring failures, and for the sake of simplicity I have written as though the relationship were exclusively a mother–child one, whereas in reality both parents are increasingly involved, in varying ways and degrees. (Naturally, a good mother substitute—nanny, adoptive or foster mother, even elder sister, etc.—can fill the same role.)

To a young child, his mother is everything—food, love, security, knowledge, life itself. At the baby stage it would be impossible to separate her role into symbol and thing, the two are fused in a total experience. As the child grows he begins to draw from all kinds of other sources the things he once got from his mother alone. Other people can give him food, he can even fetch it himself. Others can love and help him, and answer his questions, he can discover things for himself, explore

71

new experiences without her presence. But for a long time she is still the one who helps him to sort out his experiences, and judge them, and who gives him the confidence to do things for himself. At this stage then, his mother has a more symbolic rôle. She doesn't *in fact* give him all he needs, but she still *means* to him something that enables him to do and search and want and question and grow. But since she still guides his judgements explicitly, and corrects and supports his efforts, she is to that extent still also the thing symbolized, as well as the symbol. Later on, other influences also form his judgement and correct his efforts. What he learnt from his mother becomes more interiorized, more worked out and made his own, so that his judgements and efforts are his own, and he no longer needs, normally, to refer to her personally. He may often come to revise or reject some of her judgements. Yet he obtained from her, originally, the power and confidence to act and judge for himself, and she is still the symbol, in a very real but indefinable and generalized way, of life, security, knowledge and love. At this stage, then, the symbolic role and the practical one are distinct, and by the time he is grown-up the second has virtually ceased.

This, at least, is likely to be the case if the child's life develops very peacefully and successfully. Two things will alter this picture drastically. One is some personal weakness of character, the psychological equivalent of a slight physical handicap, which makes the child rely on his mother longer, and more completely, than normal. In this case the mother retains, perhaps all his life, some of the practical as well as the symbolic role of his early years. I have described this as due to "weakness", but this is in one way a bad description because to our puritanical outlook it implies a moral failure of some kind. True, weaknesses of character as of body are not ideal, but they can be compensated by the development of other gifts and qualities, so that the final result can even be more humanly beautiful and valuable than in the case of the normally developed character. We are ready to grant this in relation to physical handicaps but less ready to admit it about psychological ones. But a willingness to perceive and admire the human quality of people with such a weakness does not alter the fact that it *is* a weakness, and that it entails a degree of dependence beyond the normal, in which the mother's (or mother's substitute's) role as "thing" as well as symbol may have to be a permanent feature of the relationship in some degree.

The other thing that can alter the picture, in the case of a person who has no particular permanent weakness, is any kind of exceptional stress—illness, career failure or failure at school, loss of a loved person, or the effects of excessive fatigue, responsibility and anxiety. It also happens more briefly, in childhood, when something frightening or painful happens, such as a nightmare, a visit to the dentist, an attack by a dog, and so on. In such cases, the child or young adult will often regress dramatically in his relationship with his mother. He will suddenly and irrationally demand that she be once more, or more completely, the "thing" symbolized and not merely the symbol.

The mother may or may not be able personally to measure up to such demands for reassurance, comfort, healing and guidance. She may accept this role and do her best, or she may resent and fear it because it shows up shortcomings that were not apparent when the easier "baby" versions of such demands were made. Or she may delight in and cultivate it, and fear to lose it again, so that eventual recovery or removal of causes of stress leaves her with a grievance. The sensible mother will not be surprised or upset by being expected at times to fill a role appropriate only to a babyhood stage, but she may be irritated or amused if the help demanded is clearly quite unnecessary. For instance, a child afraid of a large dog may expect his mother, symbol of security, to provide an actual refuge from its attacks, although it is clear to the mother that the dog has no

THE EXPERIENCE OF MINISTRY

intention of attacking. More tragically, such a demand can be agonizing, when, for instance, a child or even a grown-up demands from the mother salvation from pain or death, and she can do nothing. There are so many varieties of reaction in behaviour, in such a crisis-relationship as there are mothers and children affected, but they all turn on the ability to cope— implicitly or explicitly—with the mother's rôle-shift from thing/symbol to thing plus symbol to symbol alone, and back again, and then again forwards, if and when it is necessary.

Memories of one's own childhood, and a glance at mothers and children personally known, should provide practical examples of how this works. And this process is so universal and so easy to observe that it should make it a great deal easier to understand the apparently more complex pattern of the clergy-laity relationships.

I think it should be emphasized that the parallel suggested here really is a *parallel* and not just an image. We may use physical parenthood as an *image* of the church's—and by extension the minister's—ability to "sow the seed" of faith, and "give birth" to Christians in baptism and "feed", "heal" and "strengthen" them with sacraments and the word. These images are powerful and illuminating, but they are only images, they are not parallel instances of the same kind of process. It is risky not to make this distinction perfectly clear, because it is often an inability to distinguish that produces anxiety among clergy and laity alike. So the image of the ecclesial "fatherhood" of the presbyter is looked at askance by people who are afraid this means a permanent small child– parent relationship between laity and clergy; at the same time those who value the *psychological* "fatherhood" of the clergy feel that it is being torn from them when anyone suggests that the theology of the Christian ministry does not involve this. It seems to me equally mistaken to suppose that a rôle of psychological parenthood is either inseparable from the spiritual rôle of the presbyter, or necessarily destructive of it.

74

Once this distinction is clear, the parallel may be drawn on usefully and obvious differences in the type of relationship need not confuse the issue, as they easily do when one is used as an *image* of the other. A child's mother must at first always be, and a Christian minister may often have to attempt to be, in *fact*, what their role is *symbolically*. The Christian official minister is the sign of the being-in-Christ of the Christian community, and so ministers must often, perhaps usually, try to give the practical psychological support, guidance, comfort and encouragement which each Christian needs in order to grow spiritually.

But the normal situation here, as in the parallel case, is that the more mature Christian should develop, as he "grows" in the faith, an ability to draw enlightenment and hope from his own Christ-coloured awareness of people and of the world around him. He should learn to judge and act as a Christian on the basis of the values and standards "the Church"—probably in the persons of only a handful of people—has taught him. A child learns to get what he needs from all kinds of sources, yet his mother retains a symbolic role which continues to colour his awareness of all these things and to enable, at least originally his personal decisions and acts. In the same way the Christian minister (and not necessarily a particular one who influenced a person at one stage, but actually the presbyterate as *symbol*) remains the symbol of the work of the Spirit in the Church, guiding, enlightening, supporting and encouraging. The presbyter retains this symbolic role even at times when a particular Christian feels no need of help from "outside" because he has interiorized what "the Church" has given him. The presbyter is still the symbol to some extent even when he is a personally inadequate Christian and unable to offer any but a feeble caricature, in personal qualities and virtues, of the "thing" of which he is a sign. But if his personal fulfilment of his rôle *as a Christian* (as distinct from his presbyteral one) is too glaringly inadequate and scandalous then he weakens the

75

symbolic force of his *presbyteral* rôle, just as a silly and selfish
mother weakens her own role, so that, babyhood once past, her
child is unlikely to turn to her for help and may acquire an
embittered view of motherhood in general. (And it is worth
noticing that this is by no means a small loss.) The Catholic or
high-church view in the past has often been that the personal
qualities of a minister are comparatively unimportant, provided he exercises his functions adequately. The familiar
middle-class hobby of "shopping around" for a congenial
church or minister has been decried for that reason. But the
"adequate" carrying out of the minister's official role is not a
mechanical thing, any more than one would describe as "adequate" a mother who confined her notion of a mother's job to
the physical feeding, cleaning and dressing of her child. The
"adequacy" of the minister depends to some extent at least on
the intensity of his symbolic value, and this depends on his
qualities as a Christian, though these need not be the ones
traditionally associated with the ministry—that is, those of
psychological parenthood. For instance, a really good man may
serve shiningly as the sign of the community's being-in-
Christ even though he may, for instance, be unobservant and
naive about people, or diffident and clumsy in his moral judgements, or extremely hot-tempered or tactless.

But assuming that the normal and proper situation is for the
mature lay Christian to find strength and enlightenment from
the symbolic, rather than the practical, role of the particular
minister, there will still be many occasions when the situation
will require the minister to be the "thing" as well as the sign.
There will always be some Christians who need lengthy and
perhaps lifelong support and guidance of this objective, non-
interiorized kind. Either from temperament or cultural background, they may never be able to develop the ability to see and
judge and act as Christians without constant and particular
guidance and reassurance. There just are people like this, there
always have been and there always will be. It may not be ideal,

any more than it is ideal that the poor should be always with us, but there they are. And the tendency of some clergy to dismiss them as inadequate Christians not worth troubling over is as wicked as the notion that it is permissible to "dispose" of a foetus that may prove to be physically or mentally handicapped on the grounds that the child will never be self-supporting. Dependence is not a sin, whether it be physical, mental or spiritual. There are many people whose lives are beautiful with courage and unselfish and humble love, who would go to pieces if they were not given constant support. Conversely, an ability to form good independent judgements, and to perceive the Christian reality with clarity, is no guarantee against self-righteousness, coldness and cruelty. It is not for nothing that traditional spirituality in all the main Christian traditions has stressed the dangers of those in authority and has seemed to harp obsessively on the evils of intellectual pride. We may have overdone the humility bit and tried to turn out docile Christians like a chain of submissive paper dolls, but the people who wrote treatises on the spiritual life did know a thing or two about human nature—some of them, anyway.

But that see-saw with humility/passiveness at one end and enlightened judgement/pride at the other end is bound to be a permanent feature of the Christian scene until kingdom come. And whether we like it or not there will be Christians who require their minister to be "thing" as well as sign, as best he can, and these people are neither better nor worse, morally, than their more psychologically mature and independent brethren.

But the feature of the situation between clergy and laity which causes most trouble at present is the one that corresponds to the second reason why mothers may find themselves obliged to reassume a role they had, normally speaking, outgrown. It is naturally not unusual for ordinary Christians to want more help and encouragement than usual from their minister in times of strife, doubt, and danger, and this must always impose a great

77

extra strain on men of whom so much is asked. They may or may not be able to cope, and some may give way under the strain. What is unique about the present situation is that a period of extreme stress in all the major churches is also a period when doubt is being cast on the traditional evaluation of the ministerial role. So the men of whom, suddenly, so much is demanded are at the same time weakened by doubts not only about whether they can respond but about whether it is right that they should be expected to. The combined onslaught of exterior demands and interior uncertainty is just too much for a great many, and no wonder.

Some women who were quite happy with babies fail miserably when the torments of adolescents confront them. They resent and fear problems with which they feel incapable of dealing. They may try to maintain their dignity by handing out arbitrary pronouncements (that don't meet the situation) or they may rebuff demands for help, resenting them, and feeling or saying, "He's not a baby any more. He's got to sort things out for himself. Why should I do it?" And this reaction is not due to lack of affection but to the fear of being swamped. Something similar seems to happen with many clergy. Some try to cope by pronouncing the situation coped with, and blaming any signs that it isn't on the worldliness, pride and disobedience of their flocks or of the age; but others try to avoid the clinging, begging hands, because they are afraid. And they rationalize this by pointing out (quite rightly) that theologically the Christian presbyter is not a sort of glorified nanny, and that mature Christians should be able to cope with difficult situations without running to hide behind her skirts. This is true, as it is true that the Alsation dog next door is better dealt with by a minimal knowledge of dog nature than by an appeal to Mum's protection, and that a toochache will not respond to maternal soothings but requires a visit to the dentist. But the fact remains that the dog is frightening and the tooth is painful, and both are easier to cope with if there is a sense of support in the background. Mother is the symbol of the strength and courage needed, and she can evoke these things in her children, even when she is powerless to affect the situation directly.

The same applies to the minister harassed by demands (conscious or not) that he cannot, personally, meet. He may not be able to solve the theological puzzles, provide quick answers to agonizing moral dilemmas, give truthful reassurances about the future of the Church or act as a banner for whatever reform is in view. What he can do is to enable others to draw from him the confidence to cope with these things for themselves, or the courage to endure what cannot be altered. He may or may not have the personal gifts that make him a leader in such situations; he may or may not be able to be (at least a little) the "thing" as well as the sign of the Church's being-in-Christ. But if he has not those gifts and cannot be that kind of thing, there is still nothing abnormal in his people's expectation that he will have and be these things, because experience shows that in a crisis this is what people do expect. And even if he has and is none of them he need not retreat, or camouflage his failure. He may be able to do *more* for the people through his lack of traditional "priestly" qualities than if he had them, provided he does not give up on his role as a Christian. By his own confidence and faith and love he can inspire others to do what he cannot do for them, and face that from which he cannot protect them.

He cannot do this if he is busy explaining that they've no business to expect him to do anything at all, because after all his ordination didn't make him any different from them in personal qualities. It didn't, any more than childbirth automatically makes a woman a good mother, but one can't wriggle out of a situation, once it has been entered into. A mother is a mother and her children will expect motherliness from her unless she abandons them or ill-treats them or lets them down so often that they learn to ignore her, or to hate and reject her. An ordained minister is stuck with that rôle, and the expectations it raises, unless he destroys them by consistent indifference or utter incompetence. And in both cases people are modified by their rôles, if they let themselves be, to the extent even of measuring up to unreasonable demands. If they can't measure up they can still enable others to do so, by continuing—perhaps miserably and almost despairingly—to be what they humanly are, as well as possible, in whatever rôle.

The lesson of this applies especially to the present difficult stage in the life of the Church, but it doesn't end there, because a recognition of the real nature of the situation also indicates how it may change for the better.

It will not improve if lay people continue either to demand the traditional rôle from a clergy whose traditional supports are being removed, or to deny to the clergy any role that seems appropriate to a human being rather than to a Scriptural text.

If both clergy and laity can learn to accept the limitations and virtues of their human nature, and recognize the perfectly normal and inevitable character of each other's reactions, we may gradually modify those reactions. We may learn to live with ourselves in patience and not revenge our shortcomings on each other. This is how it works in other relationships, in families and the more successful religious communities. They work because people learn to accept their own and each other's rôles, but don't worry if they aren't a perfect fit. They so seldom are, and it doesn't matter, so long as people don't get worried over it and try to alter the rôle to fit each person, or, failing that, pretend that they never should fit anyway—both equally misguided solutions. The acceptance of an imperfect fit is required, once one realizes that all important human rôles have this duality of sign and "thing". This is as old as sacramental theology, but it is less often recognized as an absolutely normal part of everyday experience.

If we can accept the situation and live with it for a while, we shall not, as some people hope, "get back to normal" by which they mean the traditional coincidence of sign and some attempt at "thing" in the ministry. But we may discover an atmosphere in which it becomes humanly possible for new patterns to develop between clergy and people. The expectation of leadership and "fatherhood" from those ordained will always be present because there will always be a need for it. But there will be room for the clergy to feel their way into other "thing" rôles as well, and for lay-people to take on, as they are already doing, some of those that have in the past normally belonged to the clergy. If this does happen it will be because a considerable cultural change has already taken place, so that the change in the role of the minister is part of a bigger realignment of social relationships. How does this kind of cultural change work its way through into the whole life of a big, and very varied, society? This experience has already been touched on in the previous chapter, since it affects all our thinking, but it needs to be examined more minutely here, in the light of the change, as it affects notions of ministry.

An example of far-reaching cultural change is one that unrolled through the eighteenth century, something called the "enlightenment". It was a climate of thought that grew to affect virtually all educated people, even though many of them couldn't have given any explanation of the philosophy itself, and would often have rejected it angrily if they had understood it. The release from medieval "superstition", the notion that the world was essentially explicable and rational (even if we had some way to go before it could be entirely understood and controlled by reason) affected everybody's thinking, from the deist or atheist philosopher, through the churchmen whose religion was stripped down to nothing much but an ethical system with social sanctions, to ordinary people who retained the outlines of traditional beliefs and behaviour patterns but insensibly adopted the "enlightened" attitude to the murkier aspects of human nature. "Everybody's" thinking; everybody, that is, who was educated, which meant everybody who could read, and whose life also provided the opportunity to read more than the Bible and those tracts considered suitable for the lower classes. In the period before the industrial revolution had created the "working class" there were, indeed, more well-informed and well-read working men in towns and villages, who could and did discuss such ideas, than the smugness of what we think is a twentieth-century achievement in popular education will normally let us realize. But the combined onslaught of industry and Methodism (the latter to some extent compensating for the spiritual impoverishment caused by the destruction of traditional patterns of living,) effectively prevented the gradual spreading of "enlightened" notions to the "lower classes" in general.

Even without this effect of social upheaval the spread of such ideas would have been slow. It is difficult to say whether among people with little effective contact with movements of thought common to the more highly educated, an undisturbed traditional pattern of thought and life is more or less effective in minimizing the effect of such movements than some drastic disruption of a way of life, affecting one class but not another. In any case, both do effectively dull the impact of new ways of thought, and in practice this means that the time-lag between their effect on the highly educated, and on the virtually un-educated, is bound to be long. Cultural movements do, eventually, reach everyone, but the length of time they take is seldom fully realized. In the case of the enlightenment, for instance, the attitude of mind in relation to science, "progress" and the secularization of religion, which hit the educated upper classes, and the more distinguished professional gentlefolk in the eighteenth century, reached the lower professional and commercial classes in the latter half of the nineteenth century, and the working classes only at the end of the nineteenth and the beginning of the twentieth. It is possible even now to talk to middle-aged working-class people who regard these ideas as "modern". (This is a very generalized and obviously sweep-

82

ing estimate of dates. There are numerous exceptions that spring to mind, but I think the speed of the movement as a whole is roughly as I have suggested.) Similarly, the theories of early psychoanalytic systems are only now generally assimilated, and recognizable in the form of axiomatic statements about human nature of a kind that cause later, more careful, psychiatric researchers to shudder. But even if the ideas are misunderstood more often than not these changed notions of human nature, of responsibility, the nature of sin and so on which psychiatric theory has fostered have by now modified the older ways of thought at the most "popular" level, in basic ways. This process has been faster than the absorption of scientific rationalism (if one can so call a movement which, at this level, is neither scientific nor rational) and has been oddly mixed up with it. The two together, with other ingredients, have indeed brought about a cultural change at all levels which is now virtually universal in the West. The spread of the psychoanalytic influence has been faster than the earlier one because education, of a sort, was more widespread by the time such ideas began to be expounded. Articles in newspapers and popular magazines helped, and later still radio and television made new ideas immediately available, even if in crude and over-simplified forms.

But availability of ideas is not by any means the only factor in deciding the speed with which cultural attitudes change. At the moment, all kinds of new discoveries and theories which may revolutionize life on this planet, notably those in the areas of genetics and ecology, are being aired through every possible medium of communication, and they are discussed among people of every level of education. Yet they have made little impact as agents of cultural change except among a tiny minority. At the more popular level they are fascinating, or frightening toys, but have no effect at all on people's basic attitudes and patterns of thinking, believing and living. This is a distinction which needs to be made because it is often supposed (and this supposition is itself a doctrine of the "enlightenment") that the spread of information is all that is required to disperse "the mists of superstition" and myth. But in so far as superstition and myth are the customs and the symbols of a whole way of life they are not altered by the mere availability of information, even when it is believed, and even when it contradicts previous beliefs and casts suspicion on the value of traditional attitudes. For what may be dismissed by the upper educational levels of society as "superstition" and "myth" when discovered among the "lower orders", will be present in their own lives under the more dignified titles of "etiquette" and "principle" or, more currently, as "decent behaviour" and "proper values". Every society has its customs and its mythology, and it is only when *these* are modified that a real cultural change can be said to have taken place. Examples of startling moves into new human territories have been early bacteriology, evolutionary theories, psychoanalysis, atomic physics, Marxism, space exploration and—most recently—what comes under the umbrella of "conservation". These can only be said to have brought about real cultural change in practice (and not merely in the mind of scientists, prophets and journalists) when they have become commonplace in the general attitudes, everyday assumptions and way of life of ordinary, only fairly well educated people.

What matters here is not what people say they believe, or what they discuss or speculate about, nor even what excites their enthusiasm. The moon-shots, for instance, roused excitement, argument and enthusiasm at every level of society. So did, more locally, the Investiture of the Prince of Wales, in a very different way. Both have some importance in popular mythology, but it is a fairly peripheral importance. Neither can, in itself, do much to modify the ordinary ways of life and thought, though both are related to areas of living which are real and important.

What matters, fundamentally, is the things people take for

granted without thinking about them much at all in the ordinary way. They think about them, and discuss them, if the notions are attacked or questioned, or if some special event emphasizes or threatens some aspect of them. Thus the Investiture evoked feelings for and against patriotism and the symbolic vitalizing function of royalty, and the moon-shots stirred up apocalyptic emotions and also reactivated a little the science-as-salvation myth. (This last had been slightly less current in recent years due to the unpleasant warning provided by the deadly Nazi use of it, and also to the revival of the much older mythology of dreams, ecstasies and the inner world.)

This very inadequate and generalized sketch of the how and what of two major cultural changes in one country helps at least to show two things. One is that important movements of thought take a long time to become general. It is only when they have become general in the sense that the assumptions behind them are taken for granted to the extent of being un-noticed that we can truly say that a cultural change has been achieved. (The most highly educated will, by then, be feeling for newer philosophies.) The other is that the "officially" re-cognized significance of a movement is no guarantee that it will matter much to ordinary people. Not even freely available in-formation is any guarantee of its acceptance as a part of life, though compulsory instruction can help, as the Russians and Chinese recognize. And at the same time subcultures which are regarded as ridiculous, superstitious or peripheral by the educated initiators of new ideas may delay or even prevent the general assimilation of big cultural movements, or may modify them by mixture with others to an extent which would make it hard for the pioneers to recognize them. The most glaring example of this is the Soviet Union, whose present culture is an extraordinary mixture of adapted ideology modified by in-eradicable popular and traditional ways of living and thinking.

If we can recognize these two factors in the process of cultural change we can learn quite a lot by applying them to our understanding of the Christian scene. Christianity is not a culture, but it is incarnate in a given culture or not at all, as I discussed in the last chapter. A faith without religious form is like a human being without language. Without words no thought can happen, though there may be amorphous emotional drives and frenzies, and instinctive trained behaviour. Without religious form there can be no faith, though there may be a blind urge towards God—we can know nothing about that. Rites, definitions, customs are the language of religion that embodies the Spirit in each man and each society, and they are not static. Religion changes, because although it is the articulation of the Spirit in man it does not and cannot do so finally and exhaustively. The Spirit prays for us, and even if his groans are unutterable we are, in religious forms, always striving for new ways to utter them. Some ways are more adequate than others. Some are ephemeral, some last for generations, but none are exhaustive and therefore none is satisfying for ever. The straining towards a better utterance is the movement of cultural change, and more explicitly of religious change.

Since religious change, like all cultural change, is a matter of language, it is not surprising that it is a minority of the highly educated which normally gives the earliest explicit expression to what is happening. Human beings are animals that speak. It is the use of language that projects man forward: the ability to articulate what is happening to him, thereby to recognize it clearly, react explicitly, and move on from there. But if the "vocal minority" scandalize the unobservant by articulating the direction of change they do not invent or initiate it. Undercurrents of change disturb the surface before anyone tries to explain what is happening. The cultural drive in the medieval Church that found a recognized form in the mendicant orders and in an emancipation from a rigidly autocratic Roman-type spirituality was there before it found official outlets, and it made itself felt also in unofficial heretical movements, and in the Romance literature. Those who articulate a cultural

86

movement also limit it by the way they find to express it.

This is happening at the moment. The movement of change in the churches was observable for some time as a sort of ground swell before it broke out. A few observant and sensitive people were aware of this, but they often misinterpreted it, because the evidence was naturally ambiguous. Among such ambiguous signs were the growing interest in ancient liturgical practices, and later the use of medieval symbolism in domestic paraliturgies; in Anglicanism the revival of medieval styles in decoration and an interest in "Roman" customs; the influence of groups of active lay Christians; the tendency among the "big" churches to move away from a traditional royalist or conservative stance in politics and to feel uneasy about the way the Vatican, or the Established Church, continued to take them for granted; a growing interest in and respect for the theology and spirituality of other churches and even of non-Christians. These things made very little impact on the lives of ordinary Christians who weren't directly affected. Lay people, for instance, formed or joined groups which undertook tasks among the poor, and the implications of this were radically new in the churches, yet these people were otherwise probably quite traditional. Again, only groups and nations whose political aspirations moved against the current of traditional Christian establishment political attitudes recognized the Christian tensions in the political area, and it didn't affect their belief or practice in other ways. And the minority who cared about a revived or reformed liturgy were uninterested in the social or political anxieties of other Christians.

But when the thing did break it quickly found voices to articulate the full scale and scope of this religious revolution. Aspects of it hitherto isolated fell into place as part of the whole, and the picture they conjured up showed the Spirit taking flesh in a religious form that few Christians found easy to identify with the Church they had known. Inevitably, the vast majority of ordinary churchgoers never noticed it at all, and certainly never as a personal option. What they saw was the alteration of little bits and pieces of their familiar church culture. Sometimes they liked it, sometimes they didn't. In any case they were mostly only interested in the things that affected their own lives—issues such as divorce or new translations of Scripture or the up-dating of the liturgy. For most ordinary Christians things were for long the same as ever, with odd exceptions, and with a new sort of anxiety in the background, mostly emanating from the clergy. The extent and continuance of ignorance of what has happened to all the churches, and why, among ordinary, church people is hard for some of the more conscious and concerned to accept. This is true both of "traditionalists" who regard the unchanged outlook of so many as a sign that they disapprove of change, and of the "progressives" who are dismayed because they suppose the same. But most people haven't approved or disapproved of the ecclesiastical revolution. They have barely noticed there is one, and this is less odd when one realizes how small is the circulation of even the more popular Christian newspapers.

New ideas are, however, getting through a lot faster than such things penetrated a few generations ago. The newspapers and TV have seen to it that Christians are constantly reminded of the goings on in their churches, and even if they have little idea of the whole picture the effect has inevitably been worrying and unsettling, and they begin to take sides. They are like tourists who wander into a square where a political demonstration is going on. They may have, when they arrive, no idea what it's all about, but they pick up slogans from placards and bits and ends of speeches or songs. The police turn up to "restore order" and the bystanders are no longer bystanders, but are forced to take sides. Which side they take is determined by a mixture of temperament, background, and the chance of what information they happened to pick up.

So it is no longer true to say that ordinary Christians are not involved in the changes, but they are involved in an unsatisfactory way, which makes them often anxious and uncertain. They are vulnerable, like the tourist caught up in a riot about which he knows nothing. Soon, some at least begin to have a more definite idea of what is going on and what they think about it, though their idea of it scarcely corresponds to the picture of which the better informed minority are aware.

Two kinds of reaction to what is going on can be demonstrated by my own encounters with two Catholics—both elderly, working-class, solid and deeply convinced Catholics. One, an English north-country grandmother, complained loudly and genially about "all this changing about of the Mass. It's not what I'm used to". And her opinions of local efforts towards Christian unity were summed up when she announced she didn't want to be united with "that lot" (with whom, in private, she was on most cordial terms!). She was an open, generous, sincerely pious woman with a sense of humour and a great liking for people—but *her* church hasn't changed. The other was a battered Irishman who buttonholed me after a unity service and, like the ancient mariner, refused to let me go until he had explained (several times over) that the Roman Church would never be healthy until Papal elections were held in public. He was convinced that jobbery was going on in the Vatican, and that to televise the consistory would prevent what he considered to be the disaster of the last election, for he had a hearty grudge against the Holy Spirit for not supplying another Pope John. This man was, if anything, less educated and certainly less well informed than the woman, he'd simply picked up different ideas in the general flurry of propaganda.

Meanwhile, the vocal minority go on being vocal, and feeling depressed because things don't move as fast as they expected. They don't move fast, unless greatly helped both by geography and by highly efficient and deliberate organization, as in Holland. And when this does happen it may well be that much is lost, for there is an inevitable emphasis on the rational which leaves little room for other, inarticulate but powerful forces to make themselves felt. Time is needed for real religious change, because this must include influences that cannot be assessed or organized by even the most efficient of representative systems.

The acute problems of discovering a new rôle and theology of ministry is therefore only one result of a general cultural and therefore religious change which is turning contemporary Christianity into something rich and strange and quite unexpected. But inevitably the problems of the ministry are at the heart of it.

This state of affairs will not last very long, in the nature of things. As one writer put it recently, the Church has voluntarily entered upon a *rite de passage* from one state of being to another. This is an uncomfortable and deeply disturbing process, and it is intended to be, for this disturbance of accepted habits and ideas is required in order to release new potentialities which, once the ordeal is over, will be used and developed in more orderly ways. But these ways are still ahead. All we know now is the disturbance, and whereas the minority have some notion where it may be leading, and at least feel fairly certain that it is leading somewhere, the majority have little assurance that anything but chaos is upon them.

Therefore in clergy-laity relations we have the two-sided problem that people require leadership as seldom before, but the normal leaders are not certain where they are going, or even if they have the right to lead. From the lay point of view, it seems that in this situation two things are desirable. One is that the clergy should try to be less worried by the varying and conflicting demands made on them. These are normal in the circumstances, and it should cause neither surprise nor guilt if many individuals are not able to measure up to them. The clergy should feel able to accept the demands, and to admit frankly when and why they cannot fully meet them. This, contrary to expectation, increases the respect and confidence people have in their ministers, but it also calls out lay resources to help the people as a whole through its difficulties. This is what happens when anyone in authority—parent, teacher, industrial "boss"—has the sense and humility to accept and admit both his responsibility and his limitations in carrying it out. The result is increased confidence, co-operation and energy all round.

The other is that better informed lay people should stop fidgeting and fussing because so many Christians aren't interested in things that seem to them so vital. If they are vital, they will gradually penetrate the consciousness of the Church, and will do so in the normal and integral way which includes a mixture of less conscious, more ambiguous influences, all of which make up the religious culture though only a few may be capable of explicit definition.

In the meantime, lay people may quite often find themselves placed in positions of leadership, in which some kind of ministry is required of them. The situation itself is what makes this happen, and it is in such unofficial ways that the future form of ministry will begin to emerge. In the apostolic Church, deacons were appointed to do a practical job that urgently needed doing. Later their status and function was further expanded and defined, and given a liturgical focus. It is too soon to tell what kinds of ministry the future may demand, and in what ways they may become a useful and accepted part of the Church's normal life, but future forms can be helped to emerge from this period of rebirth if both clergy and laity can find the faith and hope and humility to accept both the Church and themselves, in this disturbed state.

This does not mean being satisfied with the present state of affairs, but it means that real, human, valid change is the work of the Spirit. It is something we have to serve and discover, and exploit—not dictate. It is not the January sales at Harrods, nor the Conservative Party Conference, nor a California love-in. There are Christians who would like it to be one of these, and try to interpret it to fit their chosen image. The true image is neither one of frantic optimism, nor of laborious and faithful organization, nor of unstructured *détente*. The best image is that of the dance. The rhythm of this dance is the rhythm of the Spirit's movement over the face of the earth. In the dance, clergy and laity, one people move in patterns whose completeness they cannot see. They move round each other, changing places and exchanging gestures, but finally the movement is resolved and a new set of relationships becomes visible, before the dance moves on again.

We all have a place, and move freely, but in controlled relationships. Absorbed in our own role, intent on following it through its changes, we cannot normally be aware of the whole pattern. But there is one, and Christ is Lord of the Dance.

4. The Experience of Family

THE form of Christian living that emerged from the upheavals of the Reformation settled itself around two centres—the ordained ministry, and the Christian home. Just as people are asking, "What is a priest?" and "What is the ministry for?", so they are questioning the nature and purpose of the family and often attacking the traditional "shape" of family life as a restrictive environment that tends to make people dependent, possessive and defensive. Whether we like it or not, the cultural changes over the whole of society have forced change in all aspects of Christian living, and family life is no exception. It is changing and it will change. If we are to experience these changes in a positive and hopeful way we need to be aware of what is happening, so that we may judge our own experience with a Christian conscience, rather than merely reacting on the basis of unconscious prejudice or conditioning, whether negatively or positively.

"Family" is part of everyone's experience in some way. It is a complex and controversial concept, yet for most people it starts as a fairly simple assumption about something that at first sight appears to be very simple. What do we think of when someone says "the family"? Barring some kinds of reaction which arise from a deprived or unhappy childhood, most of us would produce a description something like this: this thing called "the family" consists of father, mother, and some children, possibly a grandparent as well, and also a sort of fringe of non-resident, but more or less visiting, blood-relations. All this is held together by bonds of affection of varying strengths. (If it isn't, we may feel this is rather shocking.) So far so good, and there is a sort of negative reinforcement to such a definition by people who disapprove of "the family". When people who dislike its effects denounce "the family", they help to make clear what the popular image of it is, because what they denounce is a tight little group of people held together by exclusive and compulsive emotions. This is known as the *"bourgeois* family" for purposes of denunciation, but all it really amounts to is that this form of human association is held to be destructive of freedom and true community, whether it occurs in a "bourgeois" society, properly speaking, or in some other setting.

Whether one approves of it or not, this notion of the family is the one that has come to seem obvious to us—so obvious that there are a number of things about it that we don't notice. Perhaps the greatest gap in our awareness of "the family" is our failure to realize how *unusual* our stereotype of family life really is. What is unusual is not the grouping of husband, wife and children, but the notion of *emotional obligation* implied for us by this biological grouping. Love, as the family cement, is a very unusual concept—and a very recent one. Love has always been liable to occur in families, and has generally been encouraged and approved of when it does occur, but it is only recently that it has been regarded as the *sole important means of preserving family unity*, whatever the sociological pressures that dictate its form. The most common cement has always been, and in fact still is, the plain economic one, though it is less urgent and more disguised, nowadays. In most cultures where separate family, as opposed to tribal, groups are common at all (and this is not as normal as we sometimes suppose), the cohesion of the family is ensured by the parents' need of their children's labour, and the children's dependence on their parents for livelihood, and maybe for a dowry or a bride-price. Europeans often find it incomprehensible that impoverished agricultural peoples should apparently welcome large numbers of children. But children are the only certainty that the land will be cultivated and the

94

family continue to exist. In many cultures the family group, as we know it, scarcely exists. In the "extended" family which has been studied among tribal societies and still exists in Europe in "backward" agricultural areas, there is a certain emotional vagueness about which children "belong" to whom, and property sometimes belongs to the whole tribe or clan. The structure of authority and decision may be patriarchal or matriarchal, or some kind of "co-operative" system, explicit or *ad hoc*, but in any case *economic* considerations are the ones that determine family organization.

The variety of family pattern is enormous, much too great even to be touched on in a book of this kind, so I want to concentrate on aspects of the past history of our own culture. The fact that it is at least sketchily familiar may make the effort of imagination less strenuous, and the inevitable generalizations and omissions will matter less. Here, as elsewhere, family groupings have been economically determined. Whatever the arrangement, the relationships necessary to preserve the economic fabric were underpinned by the demands of society for loyalty and obedience, for that "pietas" which can apply to family, nation, or church, according to which structure requires this kind of adhesion for its existence. *Love* could and did occur in the context of family "pietas" but it was an *extra*, and it has been at times deliberately played down or even forbidden when it might work against the preservation of the social structure. It is noticeable that disapproval of adultery, for instance, is only strong in societies where the weakening of the exclusive marriage tie would also weaken the economic strength of the family unit.

The medieval family of noble birth emphasized kinship because the system of land tenure and inheritance depended on it. (This applies roughly from the eleventh to the fourteenth century, after which the system began to fall apart.) Carefully planned marriages were intended to increase or retrieve family wealth and prestige, and no considerations of personal inclina-

tion could be allowed to interfere. Children were taught to obey
and reverence their parents, rather as if they were their parents'
feudal vassals; but the boys, at least—often girls too among the
"top" families—were educated away from home in a sort of
gold-plated servitude to another noble family. There was
clearly little resemblance here to the "Christian family" ideal
as it has been extolled in the last two hundred years or so. Yet,
in probably about the same degree and variation that we are,
these people were Christian, and among them there was probably about as much real family love as there is among us,
however different the family "pattern" and way of life.

The families of the medieval peasants were perhaps nearer to
our own notion of a family, since they mostly stayed together.
Yet they could be moved, split up, or rendered fatherless on the
orders of their overlord, their daughters married off to anyone
he chose. Nobody thought this shocking, though obvious
abuses were denounced by those who had the courage and
position to do so. When it worked, the feudal unit was expected
to provide care and protection, and expected service and loyalty
in return. The notion of the family as a group of blood relations
who were secure and unassailable, and bound by mutual affection to give each other these things was clearly not a medieval
concept. This does not mean that there were no such loving
groups—simply that they weren't necessarily expected to be
like that. The sending away of very small children or the marriage of girls of thirteen or fourteen to total strangers was not
considered unkind. Life was like that. Loyalty and protection,
in the new towns also, lay in the guild, not the family.

By the Reformation period, a different sort of family group
had established itself in what was, by then, the emerging
middle classes of the towns. It first took form in the prosperous
tradesman's, or small merchant's household, and was another
kind of economic unit. It often included apprentices and
journeymen, who lived as part of the family and were treated
much like the children of the family—who were often, in fact,

apprenticed to their father. Such a household was a viable economic unit, not dependent on land or inheritance, and therefore this sort of self-reliant, self-respecting family group was one of the institutions that survived and prospered when the medieval world broke up. It survived because, short of total national collapse, it was an economic unit that could manage without support from others. The other bonds of support and service in the medieval world ran *across* and *through* family groups, and held society together in the feudal net. Once the net broke (through such varied causes as the Black Death, the New Learning, the rise of the merchants and with them the towns, and the corruption of the Church), the future lay with those who could manage without it. The family, as a group of relations and their immediate dependants, was suddenly expected to supply all that daily life required both economically and emotionally. Outside it there was only vagrancy and the new Poor Laws.

These, then, were some of the circumstances that made necessary the emphasis on the now suspect virtues of family independence, respectability and loyalty. Here is the beginning of something like the "modern" pattern of family life. The bond is still an economic one and religion, as always, comes in to underwrite family (as well as Church) "pietas"—the virtues of filial submission and obedience, diligence and thrift which are needed to preserve this form of community. There was certainly plenty of affection in such families, but that was not what kept them together, nor was it expected to do so.

It is interesting to see, in the decline of any kind of culture, how institutions that have once been useful, and kept in being *because* they were useful, are preserved after they cease to do anything but provide a way of life for the people concerned, who would otherwise lose any sense of purpose or identity. This is done by creating a strong network of "taboos" and customs which are absolutely unquestioned—for questioning would reveal their arbitrary and irrational nature. We can see this happening in the great families of the eighteenth century. They had (long before) been the real, necessary, if often ruthless, rulers of the land. They had governed in areas where the king's power was nominal, and the country had depended on them. By the eighteenth century, however, a more centralized government, more respect for law, and the employment of professional armies meant that many of them lived off the rents from their land, but cared little for it. They did not govern, they could not or would not farm, they were not needed to fight and were useless to virtually everyone—including themselves. Some began to take an interest in trade and to invest and speculate, though they were usually too proud to do it professionally and used agents. Such families retained their sense of importance and their place in society through a deep conviction (shared by almost everybody else as well) that their very existence was privileged and important, regardless of character and achievement. This conviction of being privileged could survive even disastrous financial losses through gaming or foolish financial speculation.

Marriages were designed to reinforce this conviction of the absolute value of noble birth, and children were brought up to take it for granted that the one thing that mattered was the honour of the family name. One might hate and despise one's father or mother, or, in fact, all one's relations, but the honour of the *name* must be upheld. And what dishonoured it was not dissolute living, or vice of any kind, but marrying someone of low birth. In time, from sheer necessity of survival, this kind of marriage might be condoned if the bride were rich enough, but this was felt by the "best" families to be a humiliating surrender of pride, and a sign of decadence.

This is, perhaps, scarcely imaginable to us, and its importance from the point of view of a study of the modern family is simply that it illustrates the kind of thing that was going to happen to more ordinary families, though in a different way. For by the nineteenth century the middle-class family, too, was

98

ceasing to be a real economic unit. The "cottage industry" family group had almost disappeared into the factories, and the households of craftsmen and apprentices were becoming rare. Yet it was as important as ever for the self-respect and spiritual welfare of ordinary people that the sense of family should survive, since there was nothing else to answer to the need for support and a sense of belonging which is essential if people are to grow up with confidence and an awareness of identity. Neither the nation nor (except in traditional rural communities) the local community could provide this, for the new towns and cities had broken up old patterns, and there was little feeling of "nationhood" after a century of Hanoverians and press-gangs. The family was badly needed as a spiritual protection and prop in all classes, yet its members were, for the most part, separately employed, or genteelly unemployed if it had money enough. The "sweat-shop" system did sometimes keep families together, but virtually destroyed family life as such.

So a system of irrational taboos came into operation for the same purpose as those which preserved the mystique of the landed aristocracy, and it was during the nineteenth century that the *emotional* family bond became so important, and so much stressed. This was something more than the demand for family "pietas"—obedience and loyalty, regardless of feelings. Because there was nothing else to preserve its existence, a strong sense of *emotional* obligation became essential to family life.

This nineteenth-century middle-class ideal has acquired an absolute value in the Christian ethos, so that when we say "family" we have a mental picture of roughly this kind. This is simply a fact, it is not a value judgement. I have tried to indicate briefly how I think it happened, because it is necessary to take this image to pieces and see how it is made up if we are to go on and recognize possible future forms for the family without being hampered by a ghostly stereotype which insists on regarding itself as the only possible kind of Christian family. To show how this stereotype occurred is not to canonize it, or

99

to condemn it. It grew up because it was badly needed. It was a middle-class creation but, in the total absence of any other form of real human community, it was also the only possible salvation for the working classes. Family devotion was the one thing that could give the poor a sense of self-respect and a will to survive in appalling conditions. Novels of the period, from Dickens down to forgotten religious tracts, all show the importance of this bond in giving people the will to live, and "make good" at least in a small way. Outside this magic circle individuals were easily absorbed into a kind of limbo, beyond which gaped the doors of hell (labelled "work-house" or "prison") or—slightly less ghastly—a life of more or less successful crime, supported by the only existing substitute for family life, the criminal gang such as Dickens described in *Oliver Twist*. When we realize that this was the only tolerable alternative to the tightly knit support of the family group we realize why this devotion mattered so much, and why the obligation to love one's family acquired a religious force which has survived until now, though gradually weakened as the sheer necessity for it lessened. It is a middle-class pattern, and the middle classes articulated it, enshrined it in literature, and ensured its survival. The word "respectable" has come to have a derisive ring to it, yet at that time to be "respectable" meant to belong in a proper pattern and to have dignity. The ideal of the respectable family was a great achievement in the face of terrible threats to human life.

We can see it in novels throughout the century. In Jane Austen's novels disrespect for parents is regarded as peculiarly disgraceful, even when they don't personally deserve any great respect. Jane herself is ironic about exaggerations of filial loyalty, but assumes the essential rightness of the basic attitude. Fanny, in *Mansfield Park*, though only their daughter "by charity", still feels herself obliged to love and respect her uncle and aunt with truly filial fervour, whatever their real qualities. She also tries her hardest to feel love and respect for her slatternly and neglectful real mother, and reproaches herself because she cannot regret having left her. In *Emma*, the heroine's obligation to put her father's needs first, even when these needs are partly imaginary, is accepted as unquestionably right. Jane Austen implicitly questions the morality of Mr. Woodhouse's self-indulgent exploitation of his daughter's affection, but not the rightness of her determination to humour even the least reasonable of his whims. In *Jane Eyre* Charlotte Bronte also attacks the hypocritical abuse of the obligation of family loyalty, showing how the child Jane is justified in her rejection of her odious aunt, but Aunt Reid's accusations of unnatural wickedness and ingratitude show the assumptions of the time about the proper attitude of children to parents, or parent-substitutes. The importance of family affection as a support and refuge is apparent in many of Dickens's novels, and the need therefore to overlook parental shortcomings—Mrs. Nickleby's silliness, for instance, or Mrs. Copperfield's weak dependence and cowardice. Dickens shows the contemporary idea of the kind of quality family life ought to have at its best, in the home life of Traddles, and in the Peggotty *ménage*, the family of Scrooge's nephew, even the Micawbers' histrionic devotion to each other. But he also shows its distortions, in the idolatrous love of Mrs. Steerforth for her son, in the revolting Heaps, or the Squeers family. He points up precisely the reason why real family life mattered so much in the pathetic condition of the husband and children neglected by Mrs. Jellyby in favour of her unfortunate but fortunately distant African protégées, and even more in his account in *Oliver Twist* of what happens to children—and adults—who have no family. By the end of the century the distortions were getting more emphatic treatment, but even Butler's *Way of All Flesh* is a negative proof of the strength of the family mystique, since he, with many others, felt driven to attack it so bitterly.

This is our heritage, and though there have been rebels

against the tyranny of family devotion from Samuel Butler onwards, it remains strong, and has enshrined itself in the Christian conscience as the one, truly Christian, ideal of family life. If we now have to move on, there is no need to despise it. It was, at its best, admirable.

By now, however, we should be able to recognize that it is not the norm we once felt it to be, but a cultural oddity, resulting from a very special set of historical circumstances. It is one among many possible forms of family pattern which have worked equally well and are still doing so.

It is too easy, however, to go on from here and conclude that if *our* kind of family image is a special and probably fleeting one, then—on its departure—it does not matter what kind of pattern of family life we have. But we are not considering simply whether a certain form of family life is economically viable. There have been plenty of patterns which have been entirely successful from *this* point of view, but which have been quite unacceptable from a Christian point of view. The Samoan "extended family" worked excellently, with no strong emotional ties, virtually "free" sex, and disposal of unwanted babies by strangling. It got on well by carefully eliminating love from the system—love was just as rigorously "not done" in Samoa as in the marriages of the "Beau Monde" of eighteenth-century Europe, and for the same reason: love was liable to upset the social applecart.

For the same reason, we reject the regime of Mr. Barrett of Wimpole Street. There was much talk of filial devotion in this type of family, but the reality was a kind of moral bullying. On the other hand, the nineteenth-century pattern has commended itself to Christians, not only because it is the one they have been used to, and which was necessary, but also because it is a pattern that, at least in theory, makes the family-bond one of *love*, not economic necessity. It may have been, often, a phoney sort of love but at least it claimed to operate with love as its fuel. This matters to Christians.

If we want to recognize emerging alternatives to the traditional pattern, and judge them as Christians, we shall hope to discover a pattern in which real love can flourish. There are some in which it can, others in which it cannot, and we have to judge, and then encourage the right kind of development. In order to do this we have to decide the answers to two questions. First, what are the essential human ingredients of a pattern of family life in which real love can grow? Second, what are the existing and foreseeable social conditions we have to take into account in trying to discern which patterns for the future could make sense to us as Christians?

The answer to the first question must be familiar. We require that a pattern of family life provide sufficient (though not necessarily geographical) stability, the opportunity for healthy and full emotional development, and for growth of a clear sense of identity in its members—as human beings, as citizens and as Christians. These are required for the benefit of the husband and wife as much for the children, for spiritual growth is not something that happens until one is about eighteen and then stops. It goes on throughout life.

It may seem contradictory to demand stability and security when the Christian need is for a spiritual adventurousness, a willingness to "sell all and follow Me". But in practice the two things are interrelated. A person lacking emotional security, craving love and never certain of getting it, is self-absorbed and unable to give himself generously. But security by itself is not enough; it can degenerate into apathy and a narrow smugness. Ideally, it needs to be the sort of security which has, as it were, a built-in demand for responsiveness to the Spirit. At its rare best, the education of a landowner's son used to include the assumption that his position required him to be at the service of his tenants and their needs, and to put these above his own convenience. He might, in fact, evade this demand and prove a bad landlord, merely enjoying the property without caring for those who depended on him, but the fact remained that such demands would be "built in" to the notion of life he was given. This is a feeble analogy but, shorn of the overtones of patronage which a changed social outlook has given it, it does suggest the right kind of relation between stability and emotional security on the one hand, and poverty of spirit and responsiveness to the Spirit on the other. One can't *teach*, or *give*, conversion, self-abandonment, a sense of mission, and so on, but if they are to occur there must be, as it were, a launching-pad for the mission into the unknown, and it has to carefully build for its purpose. A family life that is either too unstable to provide the confidence and courage needed, or too self-centred to allow generosity a chance to leave the ground, is unacceptable to Christians in search of a future pattern. Stability, security, a sense of belonging, a sense of community identity—one can describe it many ways, but whatever one calls it, it is one element that we need to look for in any satisfactory pattern of family life. And, with it, the built-in demand that each person be ready to "leave his country and his father's house" and go wherever the Spirit calls. Both are required, and they are inseparable in any really Christian notion of family life.

The second question is a very big one, but it is possible to identify a few factors that have definitely altered family life as we have known it in the last few generations, and that also seem to offer us opportunities for the future, once we learn to recognize them.

Rather than trying to compress what ought to be a detailed sociological survey into a few inadequate pages, it may be more helpful to use as a model an earlier period of history which is, especially in ways that affect family life, strikingly similar to our own. This can create an imaginative picture which is easier to take hold of, because more remote from us, than the aggressive complexity of the situation we have actually to deal with ourselves. It may help us to see in what way we can make use of the changed family patterns we discern in our own time, by seeing how Christians of another era tackled a similar problem. For the creation of a family life in which faith and love can grow is the problem of each generation of Christians, and each has a different sociological pattern presented for its use. Given the existing patterns, it can use, adapt or reject them, judging their potentialities by Christian standards. And the family pattern from the past which I have chosen is remarkably relevant in helping us to judge our possibilities.

This kind of family lives in a world that is rapidly changing, in which efficient transport makes for mobility and increased emphasis on trade and the resulting cultural exchange leads to mixing of races and cultures. Its world is more or less at "peace", except for euphemistically designated "rebellions" or "troubles" in areas that seem, to most people, remote though worrying. This world is full of different and rival religions, and of philosophies aiming to displace religion. It is a world in which governments often pay lip-service to official religion but ignore its values in practice, though theoretically they treat all creeds and races alike. It is a world of class privilege, and of racial privilege (mostly unacknowledged and even emphatically denied but quite real) and of wide division between rich and poor. But it is also a world whose traditional pattern is visibly beginning to break up. Because this "world" is not, after all, the whole world. It has always been surrounded by alien peoples, but it is only when it is being weakened by cultural earthquake tremors within its own bounds that it begins seriously to fear the enemy without, and become obsessed by the terror of subversion and disloyalty. Because of this only half-acknowledged fear the young, and other "unstable elements" are a worry to politicians; interest in the occult, in eroticism, and in mysticism are great, as always at periods of disillusion and decline of cultural self-confidence.

It seems so familiar that it might be a description of our own times, but in fact it is the world in which the Gospel was first preached, the Roman world of the first century.

In this society we can discern three main types of family life, which are again curiously familiar. That of the rich is still much what it was before the crack-up began. Couples are protected from friction in marriages made for money or prestige, by the separateness of their lives. Wives are for breeding. Men look for their fun among more enterprising females, and wives, more quietly, can get their kicks on the side, also. Children are brought up by servants, boys are taught to despise women . . . and so on. This is very similar to the life of upper-class British families of the nineteenth and early twentieth century. Something similar persists even now among the very rich and respectable, but easy divorce has blurred the divisions between wives and non-wives.

The families of the very poor in the cities—free labourers, fishermen, porters and so on—have little chance to form a pattern of family life at all. The labour market and the wishes of employers, the police, or sheer necessity, push them around, wives are separated from husbands and children from parents. A "home" in our sense is something unknown. They live somewhere, if they can, but someone else decides where, and for how long and under what conditions. Family affection is a furtively snatched privilege that has no security, no future. For slaves, there is no marriage, and except by the whim of a kindly owner there is no family life at all. The children of poor families as well as of slaves—boys or girls—are available for the use of the rich and of anyone else who has a bit of money. (We have no slaves now, or so we say, but this description fits the poor of our big cities uncomfortably well. Nowadays, as then, the poor are always wrong.)

The third kind of family is that of the shopkeepers, the artisans and craftsmen, the clerks and teachers, the small merchants and people with little businesses, a reasonable independence, or not quite independence—in other words the much maligned middle class. (It is largely what we would call "lower middle class", mixed with more secure working-class families. But there is no clear dividing line, for families that are comparatively well to do come into the picture also.) We have come to think of middle-class families as keeping themselves to themselves, enclosed in protective isolation, respectable and rather prudish. These people were not. They were too exposed for that— exposed to ideas, to the moving populations, to the vagaries of the market, to the brutality of the upper classes and of the police—unless they had a rich friend. Parents often stayed together, if only because they were part of an economic unit, since the wife often worked also, but unfaithfulness was normal, especially among the poorer people who lacked the moral protection of privacy in good housing. The less well-off lived, like the poor, often in the *insulae* or blocks of flats with little privacy. Children grew up early and had to learn a trade, craft or profession. Sex was an early and not necessarily pleasant experience. Once married, young people might move a long way off, or stay on in the same house. Teenagers had little supervision in most of these families (no-one had time), they had to work and to work things out for themselves. But there was much mutual affection and support, and in the home a lot of coming and going of friends and neighbours, a literally open-door attitude to life.

The first Christian converts were mostly of this kind, though there were many among the slaves and the very poor, and even a few rich and noble. In each case—rich, poor or middling—Christian faith demanded to be embodied in daily living. For the rich, the traditional pattern would not do. It contradicted too much of the new faith. Either the faith or the family pattern had to give way—and we can see in Paul's letter to Philemon a case where the family pattern did give. The returning slave is welcomed as "a dear brother"—an unheard-of notion.

To the degraded and harried "families" of the poor the new faith brought hope and dignity. It *created* the beginnings of a pattern by its emphasis on the dignity, even for the poor, of married life. (It is interesting to realize that the beginnings of the idea of a "church-wedding", instead of the normal use by Christians of whatever rite was customary locally, arose because Christian slaves wanted to marry, and there was, of course, no civil rite for slaves, since they were not allowed by law to marry at all. So the bishops began to marry them secretly, and their union was recognized by the Church, if not the State.) The dignity of a decent marriage, which was a cliché to the respectable, was still an outrageous novelty for the poor. This is a challenge, nowadays, to the sincerity of "Christians" who demand cleanliness, fidelity and good manners from people living in sub-human conditions. A common formality does not constitute a common set of cultural conditions.

For the rich and the poor the existing way of life was altered by the experience of faith, because faith could not survive unless life did alter. Their way of living as families did not give scope for the kind of life their faith demanded. In the third case, that of what I called the "middle class" for want of a better description, the way of life was not basically altered by conversion, rather, after a while it was transfigured by faith. We learn that unfaithfulness and the prostitution of children and adolescents were forbidden (so there must have been reason to forbid them), as well as drunkenness and other "unruly behaviour", which were, and are, common among people whose standard of living is low, and who lack political power or security, but the pattern of social relationships, as such, did not *need* to alter. Its virtues were enhanced and cultivated, its vices gradually pruned away, but the pattern remained. These modest households, for instance, were quite normally hospitable; now they opened their hearts to all "the household of the faith". Paul naturally stayed in such households, as did the other apostles and travelling evangelists. The poor were welcomed, the sick cared for, the sad comforted, to the degree which each household could afford.

These homes also became centres of Christian teaching.

Would-be converts were sent there to learn about their new faith, as Apollos was invited to the home of Aquila the tent-maker and his wife Priscilla in order to be given "further instruction about 'the Way' ". And the bigger homes became liturgical centres, too—the only "churches" there were. Paul celebrated the "Breaking of Bread" in an upper room at Troas which was evidently big enough to hold a large number of people and need numerous lamps to light it. Priscilla and Aquila must have been sufficiently prosperous to have a sizeable house, for Paul refers to "the church that meets at their house" (note, incidentally, as a sidelight on social relations among these Christians that it is *their* house, not *his* house—the wife is treated as an equal). The richer members were naturally able to be more lavish in hospitality and charity—lavish, that is, in welcoming more people, for their standard of life was expected to be simple even to sparseness, though they were not to beggar themselves. As St. Paul put it (2 Cor. 8: 13–14) in talking about how much to give away to those in need, "this does not mean that to give relief to others you ought to make things difficult for yourselves. It is a question of balancing what happens to be your surplus now against their present need, and one day they may have something to spare that will supply your own need."

They were not all saints. The old vices recurred. Paul had to rebuke his converts for frequent lapses into pagan behaviour, rowdiness or arrogance. But they had their values right and they embodied these in a form of family life that was, at least potentially, warm, supporting, comforting (as it must be if love is to begin to grow), but *open*—open to God and to man. Paul classes the practice of hospitality with being "on fire with the Spirit", as qualities he wants to find in his converts. He evidently saw both in his favourite households, like "Stephanas' family who . . . have really worked hard to help the saints".

Here is a situation in which the sociological pressures, common to all, create a pattern of family life which can be made to fulfil the requirements for a Christian family. It provides a setting in which it is possible for people to feel emotionally if not financially secure, to know they belong, and which yet has a built-in demand on its members for responsiveness to God's demands, which may be limitless. In the apostolic period the demands of God might at any time include severe persecution, yet there was—and we can feel it in the more personal bits of Paul's letters—a very definite sense of emotional stability. People belonged to a particular home-community, which identified itself with the family that formed its centre. "The household of so-and-so" was not a chance group of people who happened to be inhabiting a particular house, but a real community, whose heart was a definite "biological" family, though the family did not constitute the entire household. This is the notable difference between the apostolic "household" and our present (but fading) family stereotype. In both cases there is a "biological" family living together, at least for a time, but nowadays any other people who happen to be there are normally visitors, servants or "extra" relatives, who do not have the same emotional status as "the family". In Christian households of the apostolic period the "extra" people are not really extra but are all part of the same household, which includes "the family". All, equally, belong, though naturally not all are equally dear to each other, or as closely concerned in each other's education and future.

Perhaps we could begin our search for the new form for Christian family life by thinking of it as a "household" rather than a family in the sense simply of a group of blood relations. In some grouping or other, married couples and children will need each other, in order to learn to love and to give. All that has been written in recent years about the role of married love and of parental love, in building up God's kingdom in each other stands as firmly as ever—but we may discover that it extends much further than we thought. Radiating out from that centre which is marriage "in Christ and in the

Church" we may have all manner of people who need, or appreciate, this love, whom the family can include in its circle of service and love.

Our *houses* are smaller, but our "household" in Paul's sense, need not be. It is a bond of love, not of bricks or timber, that binds such a "family", but the way people live determines the kind of buildings they want, and eventually get. If we want it, we can find, or convert, or, in the long run build homes that make it possible to share families, to spread the burden of work and child-care, to let children learn to include, not ex- clude, their fellows, by seeing how "these Christians love one another".

I am not, in this context, suggesting that the emerging "family" has to be something like the Israeli Kibbutzim, or the way of life of some Christian or other communities of families already living together and having things in common. This can work excellently, but it needs to become a more normal and accepted way of life of a whole society. While it remains excep- tional it can go terribly wrong. At the moment it seems to re- quire a special sort of motivation if it is to work humanly, for it is still an unusual "vocation", not a cultural norm. It doesn't, in fact, seem to be the only kind of family pattern which sociological pressures are tending to create for us at the moment. Such groups should be formed wherever possible, be- cause they are an exceptional but needed and inspiring example, in the same way that religious orders are intended to be and often are. But they seem unlikely to become very wide- spread in our culture in the near future, and for most ordinary Christians, now as previously, the Christian family will be formed according to whatever sociological pattern happens to form family life in general at the time. Christians need only refuse to accept the general pattern when either they have a special vocation to do something different, or the prevalent pattern makes the growth of love and holiness virtually impos- sible. This is certainly not the case in our society. Like the first

Gentile Christians, we do not need to alter the normal pattern so much as to transform it.

We are sometimes too easily panicked by changes that appear to work against Christian values. Some changes do—easy abortion, for instance, can only serve to undermine the sense of the wonder and holiness of each human life, however altruistic the motives of its supporters. But in a situation such as ours, when people are not compelled by law to refrain from what Christians perceive to be a distortion of real humanity, it may be that Christians have a greater chance to make clear the true humanness of moral standards that had come to seem, to many people, arbitrary and even cruel. Because abortion is more common, because divorce carries little social stigma, and extramarital sex is increasingly acceptable, because our society still pays only lip-service to the equal dignity of the sexes, it may be that Christians have, at last, a chance to bear witness to the truth in a way they have not been able to do for centuries.

We can show that children matter because they are themselves, not because they suit our convenience, and that handicap of any kind does not dehumanize unless we want it to. We can discover, and show, that the growth of a family is for the spiritual development of all its members, and its responsibilities, hardships and achievements belong to all. Easy divorce *could* mean that the value of Christian love and fidelity in marriage would be startlingly apparent, because not imposed by convention but inspired by faith. Another much-bewailed change, the increased mobility and earning power of teenagers, *could* mean that children of Christians would grow up confident in their parents' love, but aware, also, that all the world is peopled with their brothers and sisters, whom they and their parents can welcome and serve and love.

It is sometimes objected that for parents to be too open to the needs of others, too concerned about people in need of whatever kind, is an unjustifiable neglect of their responsibility to their own children. This is true—if we are careful to define how much is too much. To force children into sacrifices and hardships for the sake of others, which their parents may be fully willing to bear but which they themselves cannot accept, is hardly the way to bring up Christians open to the Spirit. They are more likely to turn a deaf ear to him for fear of what he may ask. But children who, secure of their parents love, are helped gradually to realize the tragic dimensions of misery and need both abroad and on the doorstep; and who also see their parents doing what they can, as a matter of course, and *as part of daily life* without heroics or over-much pious seriousness—such children will gradually take it for granted that this is how life is, and learn to take their share without fuss or any sense of ill-usage. To put one's children first sounds fine, but it does not —cannot—mean that we should try to give them "everything" before we begin to consider the needs of others. The children's need, one of their greatest needs, is to have the experience of perceiving, and responding to, the demands of God in the persons of their brothers and sisters in need. We may often give them more, in a really human sense, by giving them less of some of the things they think they want. And it isn't a new experience that "difficult" teenagers grow up and blossom spiritually when they discover that they are able to give something to someone else.

Part of the trouble with this idea of an open family pattern is that although such a thing has now and then happened it has seemed odd, exceptional, and therefore maybe a little self-conscious. This was inevitable because it was going against the notions of family life generally accepted in our society. What I am suggesting is that if we make use, as Christians, of actual but still undeveloped trends in family life, instead of trying artificially to preserve the pattern of a past age, we could make this kind of "open" family, or "household" pattern a normal Christian one. The amount of generosity, the level of responsiveness in each case would naturally vary, as it always has, but the fact of an "open", or "household" type of family pattern need not be a pious eccentricity for the fervent, but something quite naturally and routinely to be expected of Christians embarking on marriage. It could become as "traditional" as the present custom of the wedding in church, or of each family having its own home as far as possible—neither of which are universal, and both of which European Christians regard as normal and desirable. This tendency is already blessed, and even demanded, by the idea of marriage proposed to the bridal couple in the new English Catholic rite of marriage. Unlike the older insistence on procreation as the chief blessing and purpose of marriage, it sees the couple as the heart of a new Christian community, creating a home where the weak and sorrowful will be welcomed and helped. For once, quite amazingly, the official Church seems to be ahead of the general level of awareness in its understanding of the needs and direction of our society. This is how genuine theology grows from experience, judged and assimilated and made explicit in the decisions and hopes of Christian living.

Whether we like it or not, the future patterns of family life will be different. It is up to us to see that whatever they are they can become ways of living the Gospel. We shan't do that by burying our heads in the nineteenth century. We cannot do it, either, by copying any other period, because each new situation is to some extent unique. We are lucky, however, in that the problems St. Paul's converts had to deal with were to some extent similar to ours, which makes some of his experiences and comments considerably more practically relevant to us than they have been to Christians in the past fifteen hundred years or so.

It will be hard work to create a truly Christian—which means realistically loving—way of family life in the new society. It was probably even harder for the first Christians. If one reads the Epistles from this point of view, allowing them to build up an image of a new sort of Christian family, we begin to watch these people with sympathy, witnessing to the Resurrection in a sick, decadent and frightened society that desperately needed faith, hope, and love. Life was hard for many of them, few had wealth or material security, but the atmosphere is buoyant with hope and with the warm but quite unsentimental feeling that grows between people who share an exciting but dangerous undertaking. *Camaraderie* is a word that perhaps conveys the atmosphere better than the English "fellowship", which has become churchy and formal. There is an exhilarating mixture of friendliness, seriousness, enthusiasm, a certain toughness in the face of suffering, an openness to new people and ideas as well as a constant care for the weak in body or spirit. These things, through the ages, have been found in Christian groups who took the Gospel straight. It is the kind of effect we should expect to follow such a cause, because the experience of Christ leads to this kind of experience of living. In the past, it has often been necessary for families to break up if their members were to discover the real life of the Spirit. The family has acted as a deadening, restricting influence. It seems possible that we are moving into a type of culture where the experience of Christ will occur most readily in a family or rather in a "household" because its cultural shape allows this to happen if people want it.

We can see one form of this occurring in the increasingly common practice of celebrating the Eucharist in people's houses. In many places this is still so unusual as to create a slightly "élitist" atmosphere, and in such circumstances its chief use is to act as a kind of liturgical tonic. Its real place in Christian life in the future can only be gauged by seeing how it works when it has become part (not the whole) of normal liturgical fare. The most hopeful kind of gathering, for the future of the Church, is the one which is still based on locality, rather than special enthusiasms or abilities, since in most places (though not in "new towns" or industrial estates) this draws together people varied in age, class, interests, abilities and views.

The habitual meeting of a group small enough to get to

know each other, gathered as Christians, for *worship* rather than for some other prearranged purpose (such as raising money for charity, or opposing a new road development), means that their interpretation of the practical demands of the Christian faith can be allowed to grow naturally, as they grow in understanding of each other and of what they are doing. It will not be prescribed beforehand, nor will the only vaguely "committed" be excluded, but this kind of experience positively encourages a conscious assumption of the Christian vocation as a whole, in a way that large gatherings are unable to do. One reason is the obvious practical one that at this kind of gathering it is natural to stay on, and talk over anything that arises over coffee or even a communal meal. Projects can arise from this, but also there is a continuing process of education in Christian awareness, and this is probably more important, taking a long view. This is a basic kind of Christian experience, from which a truthful eucharistic theology is likely to develop, the theology of marriage, of Church and of Eucharist once more interacting.

One of the fears people have is that groups such as this foster an élite. One answer to this is that the Church is bound to have an élite of some kind, in the sense that some are always more "committed" than others. But if properly managed the household celebrations should actually lessen the tendency for an élite to isolate itself—and this is the real danger—provided groups draw in all who are willing, and make an effort to include various kinds of people. This kind of meeting makes it possible for people to recognize what they share, and get to know each other across natural barriers, precisely as Christians. This is more difficult at the parish level simply because of the numbers involved. A gathering centred on a family home makes it hard for people to be shy or standoffish.

Groups like this are not water-tight. People come and go, people "visit" and take the idea home, members "visit" each other's households, and so exchange ideas and "cross-fertilize". The abilities and insights and achievements of people with special gifts or interests could become available, if only to inspire and encourage, to a much wider range of people. Properly co-ordinated, groups of this kind, centred round and growing from liturgical celebration in the home, could revitalize Christian life, especially in towns and cities, and will do it in a normal, everyday sort of way which is what is particularly required if the future Church is to have a firm base. Response to crisis situations can only be good if the basic everyday life is healthy. Contrary to some fears, the spread of house-masses should not weaken the parish. It will lead to a considerable alteration in the pattern of parish life, with the parish church becoming, perhaps, a place for occasional celebration and large meetings rather than the normal thing, but this might in fact strengthen, rather than weaken, the *reality* of the local (parish) church, since the people who gathered for the occasional big celebration would be people normally and seriously engaged in liturgical and other activity at the smaller household level, each bringing their varied experience and glad to share and celebrate it with others. In this way, the parish (and the diocese, on a larger scale) would be the way these groups co-operated and grew, together and separately. A series of little cliques is the last thing we want, but a loosely but efficiently associated series of varied groups is just what is needed. Families normally have to accommodate varied abilities and degrees of enthusiasm, and the "open" family makes cliqueishness less likely. The experience of the early churches shows how well it can work.

Much depends, of course, on the availability of clergy, and this kind of decentralization could lead to a new kind of pattern of ministry.

It happens often, in groups of this kind, that one person gradually emerges as the natural leader and focus. It could be sensible to ask such a person if he (and one day perhaps, she?) were willing to be prepared for ordination, with the clear prospect of continuing the same functions in the same place, but with the added impetus of ecclesial recognition. This way of

THE EXPERIENCE OF FAMILY

choosing people for ordination would not conflict with the
preparation of younger men who, from the start, look to the
ordained ministry on their life-work. They (celibate, probably)
would still provide the comparatively mobile type of apostle
who is so much needed, and the members of group ministries
whose enormous possibilities are only just being discovered.
The two kinds of ministry would complement and assist each
other in reaching more people and kinds of situation than one
type alone can cope with.

The more flexible family pattern is already indicating a
future for some kinds of religious life. It will probably become
evident before long that the larger "mother-house" type of
community is and always will be necessary for training, for re-
training, for rest and recuperation, for periods of *détente* which
everyone needs, and to do some things that small communities
cannot manage. But it is becoming common for a handful of
men or women to live in communities (whether of Sisters, or
Brothers, or members of secular institutes, or a mixture of these
and of lay-people—the distinction is becoming less and less
clear cut anyway), doing outside work like members of a family.
This type of "family" (which turns out to be not all that
different from the type of "household" already described) provides an excellent setting for the liturgy. It could begin and
foster such development and generally act as a co-ordinating
and consolidating influence in the local Christian community.
This should help the spiritual life of its own members, as well
as providing a greatly needed "punch" of enthusiasm and support for that of families and individuals who are attempting to
create "churches" of the flexible, apostolic type, including the
communal type of family life.

A problem the apostolic household churches did not have to
deal with is one that the modern version finds itself immediately involved with. The divisions between churches pre-
occupy many Christians, but a household of the open kind will
often include people with different denominational origins.

But even if older members of the family are aware of this as a problem it must always be more natural to include these people in all that goes on, including the liturgy, than to exclude them. Exactly how the mixing goes on is bound to vary, but mixing there is and will be. But where the present younger generation is concerned there is very little awareness of the divisions, at least as a problem. The young Christians who take their faith most seriously are the ones least likely to see any sense in denominational divisions. If they find themselves in a group of other Christians they will normally worship together if they worship at all, and that includes taking communion, if a Eucharist is celebrated. This is not an act of defiance, it is simply that the arguments against it, and the prohibitions, make so little sense to them that they set them aside without even noticing it, and without any sense of rebellion. But whereas in a "proper" church building this must seem to others an act of aggressive defiance, in a home it is scarcely noticeable.

This is simply how things are, and this tendency is likely to increase, whatever anyone thinks about it, but the experience of house-centred churches should make it easier and less controversial. The new generation of Christians inherit the whole Christian "thing", and in many cases it can seem as if it itself were new. This is a real and exciting experience. They are not taking over where their elders leave off, it is rather as if two thousand years of Christianity were offering itself to them to make something of. They see more (and less) than the little bit that engaged the interest of their immediate elders. This is partly due to the increased interest in Eastern religions and mysticism generally, partly to an emphasis on *human* values, among Christians and non-Christians, and partly to the more normal intercourse between Christian traditions. They recognize and value and embrace the Christian vision, but they feel they have to discover for themselves what is actually "says" and what it demands of them. For them, the enclosing of liturgy in a particular building and time seems artificial, so here, also, the household, of some kind, is the place where Christianity is lived, if it is lived at all.

Families that normally keep open house to friends of their own children, or any other people who need help or friendship, will not find it hard to include them, after a time, in regular meetings if they are interested. Discussion among all these people can arise naturally, and a whole educational effort be generated by the demands of the situation, rather than by a "fiat" from above. This is how real understanding emerges. This is the real nursery for Christians of the future, growing from the contemporary experience of family.

The experience of family seems, when it is interpreted as a theological reality, immediately to transcend blood ties and to provide a means both of understanding and of creating a type of Christian community which is viable because it grows out of an actual situation which is accepted and understood. Left to themselves, sociological pressures do not and cannot create a church, but if a church is to be more than a self-conscious and self-created clique it must allow its life to develop out of the sociological and cultural situation. It can try to separate itself from all secular influence, and believe it has succeeded, but it cannot really do so. The breath of the Spirit, however, is needed to bring the life of Christ to birth in every kind of arrangement of human relationships, and this is the task of the individual Christians who are looking for the way to be the church in this time. The quality of the experience of family, ministry or community as *Christian* phenomena—not just ones with a given sociological shape which happens to be made up of Christians—depends on the spiritual vitality of the Christians who make it up. This vitality is fundamentally linked to sexual experience, and sexuality is part of our "spiritual" life, if it is fully understood. The next chapter therefore tries to understand more deeply the nature of sexual experience as spiritual, and this in turn demands the examination of "spirituality" itself, as a contemporary experience.

5. The Intuitive Experience of Sexuality

THE nature of an important human experience is apprehended at many levels, and the attempt to interpret them must draw on knowledge obtained by means other than purely intellectual. How this works in practice has become evident in the attempt to understand the nature of community as a Christian thing, and within that context the experience of ministry, and of that curious cliché, "family life". But these attempts inevitably raise questions about the nature of the knowledge on which we draw, and this chapter which digs into the spiritual experience of sexuality does so by way of one kind of knowledge whose existence is often neglected, and which is sometimes regarded rather as a weakness than as a help or a gift.

Intuition is, by definition, a direct kind of knowledge, whereas knowledge acquired intellectually is indirect, it has to suffer at least one translation in the process, and often many more. The unsatisfactoriness of the intellect as a tool is the refrain of mystics and poets, and the occupational hazard of scientists and philosophers. Yet intuition is not normally regarded as of much practical use. The old joke about a woman's intuition being a way of proving she's right when she knows she's wrong is not so unjust, because what we know intuitively we have to translate by means of the intellect before we can make use of it, and in the translation is inevitably distorted by all sorts of unconscious motives and half-conscious preconceptions. But these factors which make intuitive understanding more often a disturbance than a clarification are perhaps accidental. We can conceive a state of affairs in which intuitive knowledge could be a normal and satisfactory means of understanding and even of communication.

121

It is difficult in our self-consciously (and deceptively) rational culture to make use of what can be learned by intuitive understanding, quite apart from the inherent difficulties I have mentioned, but in itself intuition need not be a second-best. It may be the nearest thing we can experience of a manner of both knowing and communicating which is proper to man. Whatever is the exact nature of the experience we refer to as the "fall" of man, its effect must clearly be to muddle up his emotions, his body, and his mind to such an extent that the human brain could not be a fit instrument for making use of a direct and wordless knowledge whose vestiges we call intuition. But I am therefore suggesting that the human intellect, of which we are so proud, may be in fact a sort of evolutionary compensation for the loss (or the non-achievement?) of a more perfect kind of knowledge—knowledge of God, and of man, and of the rest of creation. If the intellect is a crutch rather than a crown then the attempt to get some help from the latent intuitive powers which are present though elusive is only an acknowledgement of the real priorities.

As a rough definition I would suggest that intuitive knowledge is knowledge which is partly an instant reaction *to* or *by* deeply absorbed symbols, including perhaps archetypal racial symbols, and partly something of the nature of telepathy or "second-sight", though these imply a much more precise kind of awareness than most people have. Whereas we usually think of people gifted in these ways as having something "extra", it helps if we think of those who are more reliably intuitive as the normal ones, and ourselves as *lacking* something. If so, intuitive understanding may be able to give us some of the light we need on significant aspects of human life, but how do we set about discovering what intuition has to tell us?

Intuitive understanding has to be translated into intellectual terms, pinned down in words, before it can be passed on, or even definitely appropriated by the person who becomes aware of it, and in the process of translation it is subject not only to personal emotional influences but to social and cultural ones as well. On the other hand these social and cultural influences are to a great extent shaped by hopes, fears and supressions which can only be experienced intuitively, so if we can locate them they should be of some assistance in interpreting the discoveries of a personal intuition.

In the nature of things a formulation of intuitive understanding is only verifiable by the internal assent of some other person who hears it. "Cor ad cor loquitur." A person who is temperamentally suspicious of intuitive experience will probably find an attempt to formulate it merely repulsive. Personally I think this reaction is evidence of a kind of sickness, but it is far from uncommon, and is usually a matter of pride to those who suffer from it. (But then there are also people who boast of lacking an ear for music, or regard their indifference to art as evidence of virility or even of moral worth.)

It may be as well to try to distinguish carefully between intuitive and emotional response to experiences. Intuitive response comes first, the emotions react to it, but although the intuitive understanding and response comes from an area too deep in the personality for lies to be possible, emotions motivated by obscure needs may quickly distort and even contradict its findings and intellectualize them. (Hence, among other things, the great muddle over the question of birth-control.) There must be a great range of human preoccupations to which our intuitive responses may be at variance with our rational or emotional ones, but I have chosen here to ask some questions (inevitably open-ended) about the area of human sexual experience, for it affects everyone, and acute contemporary moral dilemmas arise from it. The "meaning" of sexual relationship and of sexual intercourse is endlessly discussed, and is classified in categories ranging from that of simple physical appetite and satisfaction, through man's need for play and pleasure, to the romantic categories of passion and transformation through sublimated desire. To understand this experience theologically, and make it contribute to a renewed understanding of Christian life, we need more than a purely rational approach.

Several large books could be written on the subject of the intuitive valuation of sexuality. In order to remain manageable, but keep to the heart of the subject, it seemed useful to turn for help to those people who have less of a "block" to their awareness of what their intuitive knowledge is telling them, and the greatest ability to translate this knowledge and communicate it to others. These are the poets.

All the arts are means of communicating an intuitive type of awareness. Music is too close to the thing itself to be useful in interpreting intuition to the intellect. The interpretation has to be interpreted, and good musicians hate to do this, quite rightly. Painting and sculpture make a complex appeal; they speak partly to the intellect which can grasp the overt meaning of the forms, partly—under cover—to the intuitive understanding, which responds to both conscious and unconscious symbolism, and partly to the emotions, which respond to the associations of form, colour and representation. But although the visual arts are a means of intuitive communication between the artist and the beholder their full message cannot be passed from one to another, for each beholder reacts according to his own temperament and history. They have to be translated into words, which, to be a bearable (though always inadequate) translation, must have something of the nature of poetry. But poetry of its very nature makes the attempt to communicate a partly intuitive understanding. It does this by using the "insides" as well as the "outsides" of words, making them ring down the unmapped avenues of the mind and wakening echoes in rooms of whose very existence we had been unaware. But poetry can only communicate intangible experience effectively within an existing framework of myth. It is in fact the myth that matters, but poetry is the vehicle by which the myth is renewed from generation to generation, for, as Alvarez has said, the poet's job when he is really serious is to face the full range

124

of his experience with his full intelligence; not to take the easy exits of either the conventional response or choking incoherence.

My examples here must necessarily be limited, and I have therefore made use of material which was familiar to me and which I liked, or which seemed especially relevant. But if some of my quotations seem almost *too* familiar this is not accidental. The poetry that finds a permanent place in the anthologies does so, in many cases, precisely because of the deep response it continues to evoke from readers. The reasons they give to themselves for liking it are as many as the people who read, but I suggest that the real reason for the persistence of certain poetry is that it arouses an intuitive assent in the reader, though he may not understand why it pleases, and might even reject it if he knew.

I, personally, set out on this search for evidence without any preconceptions at all about what the evidence would prove. Although there is no fool-proof way of reaching the truth, this way seemed more likely to allow intuition itself to work on the material. In the end I found the destination to which I was led very surprising, but I have presented the material and its implications just as I discovered it. To help the reader to approach the material with as little prejudice as possible I have not included the poet's names, though some are unmistakably recognizable.

The first question I asked of the intuitive understanding, speaking through the mouths of poets, was: What do you *hope* that sexual intercourse will do for you as a human being? This bypasses for a moment the apparently obvious answer: the immediate satisfaction of desire, but I shall come back to it.

> Now, as in Tullia's tomb one lamp burnt clear,
> Unchang'd for fifteen hundred year,
> May these love lamps we here enshrine
> In warmth, light, lasting, equal the divine,
> Fire ever doth aspire,

THE INTUITIVE EXPERIENCE OF SEXUALITY

And makes all like itself, turns all to fire:
But ends in ashes; which these cannot do,
For none of these is fuel but fire too.
This is joy's bonfire then, when loves strong arts;
Make of so noble individual parts,
One fire of four inflaming eyes
and of two loving hearts.

And by the same man:

The phoenix' riddle has more wit
By us; we two, being one, are it;
So to one neutral thing both sexes fit.
We die and rise the same, and prove
Mysterious by this love.

And this curious result of a spell involving the catching of a
little silver trout:

When I had laid it on the floor
        I went to blow the fire aflame
But something rustled on the floor
        And someone called me by my name:

It had become a glimmering girl
        With apple blossom in her hair
Who called me by my name and ran
        And faded through the brightening air.

Though I am old with wandering
        Through hollow lands and hilly lands,
I will find out where she has gone,
        And kiss her lips and take her hands;

And walk among long dappled grass,
        And pluck till time and times are done
The silver apples of the moon
        The golden apples of the sun.

Here are the main themes—the hope is immortality, the means is some kind of experience described, over and over again, as a "burning". The great myth themes are here already, and offer us the Phoenix and the Hesperides.

The next long quotation has so much in it that it becomes my key to the mystery. It is helpful here because it is much more explicit than the others, and the author obviously thought, when he wrote it, that he had almost got what he hoped for and was certain of reaching it. Two myth themes—the eternal food and the transformation through fire—are evident here. In order to keep the extract to a reasonable length I have been obliged to leave out parts of it and so insult the poet:

> But then came another hunger
> Very deep, and ravening;
> The very body's crying out
> with a hunger more frightening, more profound
> than stomach or throat or even the mind;
> redder than death, more clamorous.
> The hunger for the woman. Alas
> it is so deep a Moloch, ruthless and strong,
> 'tis like the unutterable name of the dread Lord,
> not to be spoken aloud. . . .
>
> I thought it was woman, indiscriminate woman,
> Mere female adjunct of what I was.
> Ah, that was torment hard enough. . . .
>
> A woman fed that hunger in me at last.
> What many women cannot give, one woman can;
> so I have known it.
>
> She stood before me like riches that were mine.
> Even then, in the dark, I was tortured, ravening, unfree,
> Ashamed and shameful and vicious.
> A man is so terrified of strong hunger;
> and this terror is the root of all cruelty.

127

This comes right at last.
When a man is rich, he loses at last the hunger fear.
I had eaten of the bread that satisfied. . . .

Yet something remains.
What remains in me is to be known even as I know
I know her now: or perhaps, I know my own limitation against
    her.

Plunging as I have done, over, over the brink
I have dropped at last headlong into nought,
plunging upon sheer hard extinction;

I have come, as it were, not to know,
died, as it were; ceased from knowing; surpassed myself.
What can I say more, except that I know what it is to
surpass myself?

It is a kind of death which is not death
It is going a little beyond the bounds. . . .

It is the major part of being, this having surpassed oneself,
This having touched the edge of beyond, and perished, yet
not perished.

I want her, though, to take the same from me.
She has not realized yet, that fearful thing, that I am
the other,
she thinks we are all of one piece,
It is painfully untrue. . . .

when she is slain against me, and lies in a heap like one
outside the house,
when she passes away as I have passed away,
being pressed up against the *other*,
then I shall be glad, I shall not be confused with her.
I shall be cleared, distinct, single as if burnished in silver. . . .
Then we shall be free, freer than angels, ah, perfect.

The echo in the last lines of Christ's words about the life of resurrection is clear here: there shall be no marrying or giving in marriage—they shall be like the angels. This poem links in the mind with the end of one which isn't—or didn't intend to be—about sex at all:

> Flesh fade, and mortal trash
> Fall to residuary worm; world's wildfire, leave but
> ash:
> In a flash, at a trumpet crash,
> am all at once, what Christ is, since he was what I am,
> and
> This Jack, joke, poor potsherd, patch, matchwood,
> immortal diamond,
> Is immortal diamond.

This is the cry of passion for God, not for a woman, yet it does have the same theme as the poem that began with such a ruthless description of what appears at first sight to be nothing but a sheer physical appetite. This, then, is what some poets hope for from sexual intercourse; ultimately, nothing less than a completely perfected immortality—which includes no sex, though a burning up in union is the way there.

Now this hope crops up in poetry all the time, but it is clear that in practice, this hoped-for state doesn't occur in this world. The intense awareness of this goal is, however convincedly expressed and affirmed, only momentary. Sexual intercourse does not, in practice, lead Tristan and Iseult to what the poets say and believe that it will, but only back to the Day, after the Night in the forest, the life in the enchanted cave, is over.

What is the reaction of the poet to this dismal fact?

Here is the reaction of the author of the long, analytical poem I quoted just now—to which I shall refer again.

> I am worn out
> with the effort of trying to love people

E

and not succeeding.
Now I've made up my mind
I love nobody, I'm going to love nobody,
I'm not going to tell any lies about it
and it's final.
And if by a miracle a woman happened to come along
who warmed the cockles of my heart
I'd rejoice over the woman and the warmed cockles of
my heart
so long as it didn't all fizzle out in talk.

After the ecstatic assurance of "Manifesto" this is back to
reality—or is it? Another one is just as darkened, but ends on a
note of hope, it isn't so "final".

> When a man can love no more
> and feel no more
> and desire has failed
> and the heart is numb
>
> then all he can do
> is to say: It is so
> I've got to put up with it
> and wait.
> This is a pause, how long a pause I know not,
> In my very being.

If you put these two little poems with the long, ecstatic one,
it becomes obvious that both the original aspirations and the
inevitable darkening of vision are closely paralleled in the
writings of the great mystics. "Upon my bed by night I sought
him whom my soul loves, I sought him, but I found him not.
I called him, but he gave no answer."

But this resignation, this willingness to wait, is unusual. The
more usual reaction is, on the conscious level, a refusal to
recognize the reality of what was once glimpsed. For instance,
these remarks by a father to his son:

In Plato's dreams was this idle fancy begun—
He called you immortal, a creature sprung from the sky.
. . . But if you would know what you are, why then, you began
Your life is unquenchable lust and a drop of shame.

That is a translation—I have no Greek, which I expect puts the matter more bluntly. The fact that this particular conflict is no new thing is worth noting; this poem dates from the fourth century B.C. The next is equally downright.

> Sin I fro' love escaped am so fat,
>   I never thenk to ben in his prison lene;
> Sin I am free, I counte him not a bene.

To affect to despise or disbelieve in what you cannot attain is common form—"sour grapes" in fact. But the longing that made the first glimpse of the beyond, the "other", possible, is still there. Sometimes the attempted solution is the Don Juan one, the feverish chase from one love to another.

> Chang'd loves are but chang'd sorts of meat,
> And when he has the kernel ate,
> Who doth not fling away the shell?

But obviously, you get hungry again, for this way refuses to recognize anything further than immediate satisfaction. But, underneath, the old desire remains:

> Some that have deeper digg'd love's mine than I,
> Say where his centric happiness doth lie:
> I've lov'd and got, and told.
> But should I love, get, tell, till I were old,
> I should not find that hidden mystery.
> Oh! t' is imposture all;
>
> So lovers dream a rich and long delight
> But get a winter-seeming summer's night.

So it is inevitable that the vast majority of love poems are con-

cerned with the business of making the most of something
fleeting—youth and love, which go together.

This, whether it involves an outright rejection of social
morality, or merely seems to by-pass it, is a sort of hidden
double-talk. It says, outwardly, there's nothing to all this but a
healthy natural pleasure—let's enjoy it, while it's there, and
then try to be content without it. But underneath, and every so
often pushing it's way out, is the unquenchable assurance that
sexual love does have a significance beyond that fleeting pleasure. A contemporary poet, at a time when the conscious sexual
doctrine exalts the "naturalness" of uncommitted "cool" sex,
finds a different view forced on him by a sensitivity to personal
truth. In a poem that confesses his own ability to "pose" in
bed, as what he calls the "magnanimous pagan", he becomes
sickened with the "tragic game". Why tragic? Presumably because it is a failure of the heroic, futility where there should be
meaning. He finds himself longing for something real, and in a
revealing image of sleep after sex as death (with pennies on the
corpse's eyes) his wakened (resurrected) mind knows what is
wrong and he dismisses the false, even while recognizing the
lasting falsity in himself. It is a poem in which despair is the
necessary diagnosis that makes a cure possible. Here are the
last two stanzas:

> I hardly hope for happy thoughts, although
> In a most happy dreaming time I dreamt
> We did not hold each other in contempt.
> Then lifting from my lids night's penny weights
> I saw that lack of love contaminates.
> You know I know you know I know you know.
>
> Abandon me to stammering, and go,
> If you have tears, prepare to cry elsewhere—
> I know of no emotion we can share,
> Your intellectual protests are a bore
> And even now I pose, so now go, for
> I know you know.

The "stammering" is the effort of the half-dumb intuitive recognition to express something real about what sex is for. The earlier poet, less hampered by a legacy of doubt about the possibility of sex being "loving" at all, lacks the stammer but may sound even a little too lucid and certain as his lovers, in motionless, sexless communion, reflect.

> This ecstasy doth unperplex
> (We said) and tell us what we love;
> We see by this it was not sex.
> We see, we saw not what did move:
>
> When love with one another so
> Inter-animates two souls,
> That abler soul which thence does flow
> Defects of loveliness controls.
>
> We then, who are this new soul know
> Of what we are compos'd and made;
> For the atomies, of which we grow,
> Are souls, whom no change can invade.

The other reaction to the perennial disillusion about the possibility of love is to recommend that we——

> —Drag our pleasures with rough strife
> Through the iron gates of life.

But that is in fact a counsel of despair and so the same poet in another place complains that *true* love is

> —begotten by despair
> Upon impossibility.

And therefore:

> As lives, so loves *oblique* may well
> Themselves in every angle greet
> But ours so truly Parallel
> Though infinite can never meet.

Therefore the love which us doth bind
But fate so enviously debars
Is the conjunction of the Mind
And Opposition of the Stars.

In other words, you can have sex without love, or love without sex. But the poets go on wanting both. The original demand that the poet makes of the experience of sexual intercourse is not met, but the hope persists, in spite of protestations to the contrary. In reading and reflecting on poetry, and the recurring myths that it embodies, two apparently contradictory forces are discovered. The first is a fairly obvious one: lovers long for a complete—and impossible—fusion of personalities. They "desire to be truly each other", as Sir Thomas Browne says, "which being impossible their desires are infinite, and must proceed without possibility of satisfaction". Much poetry is an expression of this sense of impossibility.

But if we look more closely at these and similar expressions of this desire, something other than mere impossibility emerges. The desire "to be" the other is rather a desire to distinguish elements of oneself in, or over against, the other. It seems to me that this is an important part of the meaning of sexual intercourse. The longing for fusion—becoming "one fire" is in fact a stage on the way to the *other* end of sexual intercourse, which is completeness, distinction, knowledge of the self, in its own burnished perfection. But at the same time this very separateness is the condition of true union. Hence the contradictory forces that are the agony lovers; the longing for union and the need to fight for autonomy, the suspicion of false unity in sex and the fear of dishonesty in surrender.

Now it is the unitive aspect of sexual intercourse which is usually stressed, but it is the distinguishing function of sexual love—and of the individual act of intercourse within the short or long-term relationships—which is of particular interest here, because it links something essentially temporary to something eternal. Marrying and giving in marriage is for this life only.

The battle to free, discover and truly know *oneself* is then perhaps the most important thing that poets demand from sexual intercourse and the thing they most easily despair of. The myth is right—the lovers are always apart in fact, however close their bodies may be. They *must* be apart, like Tristan and Iseult, if they are to come to true union—which can only be fulfilled through death. It is not for nothing that sexual intercourse has been described as a "little death" because from this point of view it has something of the function of death—it separates in order to unite. The love-making that precedes coition is, from this point of view, an assertion of separateness, of the personality of each lover over against, even if at the service of, the other, so that in the moment of "death to self" they may come together. Possibly this accounts for some kinds of compulsive promiscuity. A person may feel unable to find and distinguish himself with one permanent partner because the other's demands, as a person, are felt a threat to personal autonomy. Yet he, or she, is still possessed by that need to "die" to himself, to distinguish himself, and so seeks various partners against whom that distinction may be hammered out. But it doesn't work, because a final act of willing submission to the union that "kills" is necessary if the personality is to die truly, and so win through to a greater degree of self-possession. This element of willingness is essential. It is what is lacking in the union that needs a dream to give the sense of death.

The assertion of separateness in love-making is not enough if that same separate person is not then blindly submitted to the momentary annihilation of a union out of which a further definition and "burnishing" is achieved, only to be submitted to a further distinction.

It is not just by chance that the language in which poets express the personal reality of loving sexual intercourse is the same in which mystics and prophets and Scripture itself have expressed the reality of conversion, of prayer, of mystical experience of God. The goal is in fact the same one, and the process is at least parallel, although the agent may be different. The goal is a distinctness of personality which will at last make a real, *complete* union possible, because beings who are not completely themselves (are indeed dissipated and confused) cannot be fully united. There will be larger or smaller bits of themselves that are not "selved", unpossessed, and therefore incapable of being given. Because this is the goal, and because the physical body and mind, in their state of confusion and imperfect self-knowledge, are an obstacle to it, the poetry of love-as-passion is forced to put an artificial (spatial or social or moral) distance between the lovers. And the Romance tradition throve on love that was sexually frustrated. Love-as-passion is forced to look for its completion in something beyond the satisfaction of the flesh. The idea of a purely spiritual love was touched on in the poem that referred to true love which "truly parallel, though infinite can never meet". But I believe modern mathematics does make parallels meet—so Tristan and Iseult *are* united—by way of death.

It is to be noticed that none of the poetry I have so far quoted or referred to so much as mentions procreation. Even the great Scriptural celebration of sexual love, *The Song of Songs*, does not refer to offspring, in spite of the Jewish preoccupation with fertility. It almost seems as if, from the point of view of those who look for the deepest significance of sexual intercourse, procreation is a side-issue. It begins to seem that this function of sexuality—the gradual, essential distinction of personality—is by its nature contraceptive, taking that word in a purely descriptive sense, without any value judgement attached. And I believe this is right, in that the physical purposes of human sexuality are only temporal, whereas its psychological ones are, in their effects, eternal. And these effects are typified in the vocation to consecrated virginity. The vocation of baptism is a vocation to virginity. This is what Durwell says in his book *In the Redeeming Christ*:

"The whole Church has been baptized in Christ's death. But that death, though real, is only the principle, the seed, of a total death, and the faithful still live in fact in an earthly body. That is why earthly love and pleasure are still lawful and can be holy, for the believer, being immersed in his body in baptism and in the Holy Spirit, shares even in this life in the holiness of his glorified body; all bodily realities have become Christian, and can belong to the new world in which we are dead to the sinful flesh."

"By baptism the Christian is raised with Christ; with him he is dead to the flesh and born to the life of the Spirit. . . . The baptized man . . . will never again be able to give his body over to any purely earthly love, for he is subject to a law of holiness, of kingly love, which is bearing him towards perfect self-giving."

"The Spirit", he says, "abolishes the flesh in us. He does not set himself against the body, for that too is created by the Spirit, but he does see himself against 'the flesh'—for these are contrary to each other—because 'the flesh' is man closed in upon the weakness and selfishness of his material being, the man of this creation who will not give himself to the Spirit. He must die to this earthly 'impenetrability' and rise again to the Spirit who is love in its fullness."

And the end of this chapter on the meaning of virginity in the Church, he sums up thus: "For all believers, the Christian life is a long process of 'virginization', its mainspring is the sacred body of the dead and risen Christ, to which we are united by baptism and the other sacraments. In marriage, man and woman are given to each other, by Christ, to be pure; in other words, to love each other, for purity which is set against the rule of the flesh is simply real love. But by calling some of his followers to virginity, Christ wills to make them a prophecy of the Church as she will be when she has attained the goal of her redemption, the eschatalogical image of the Christian in whom the mystery of the Church, Christ's paschal bride, is accomplished."

It seems to me that these passages are expressing, in theological and Scriptural terms, the nature of the experience which the various poets I have quoted are also trying to express. The traditional theologian starts from revealed truth, and tries to discover the true rapture of human life in this light, but without losing touch with actual experience (itself a theology of experience), while the poet starts with human experience and tries to express its deepest desires and hopes—but they both end up by describing the same thing.

But it is not enough to say that the intuitive experience of sex shows it to be a means whereby the Christian may die to himself and finally achieve completeness in love. This may be a valid theological interpretation, but it is not enough because it simply leaves out the other inescapable fact about sexual intercourse, which is that it is capable of producing babies. The poets may be lifted to a momentary awareness of transcendent reality beyond sexual love, but they have to come down from Mount Sinai, and the effects of that descent can be spiritually disastrous, as we have seen.

Nothing is solved by trying to pretend, as some "spiritually minded" Christians have done in the past, that sex is a purely utilitarian matter, to be ignored as far as the "spiritual" life is concerned, even by married people. Nothing is achieved by pretence—by the virgin pretending to be unsexual or the married pretending to have solved the problem merely by having sexual intercourse as a matter of duty or "legitimate" pleasure. In both cases it is the willing—that is, loving—submission to the necessities of one's state of life in relation to one's sexuality that brings about the repeated "dying", and leads ultimately to the total death, the complete liberation of the real self.

For married people that submission involves procreation.

It is rather surprising, at first, that very few poets have had anything to say about this. Poetry seems to have suffered from a difficulty in making a significant link between the high vocation of sexual love in its transforming and prophetic aspects and its marvellous but apparently essentially earthly function of procreation.

There are many poems about falling in love, and poems about wedding nights—which seldom mention conception—and poems about motherhood and even fatherhood. But poems about procreation seem to be hard to come by, and when it is mentioned it is usually with distaste. Shakespeare exhorted his young man in the sonnets to reproduce himself, but apparently only because he didn't like to think of that handsome face vanishing forever, and the process involved he seems to have regarded as a distasteful necessity—at least in that context.

Some poets—Donne for example—have transferred to married love (and by implication to the procreative function) the myths that are usually applied to love-as-passion, which is not normally thought of as conjugal precisely because it demands a separation between the lovers. So when the transference is made it sits uneasily on the domestic hearth, in fact it doesn't seem to fit in at all. Some more recent poets came to a procreative sex by way of cosmic fertility. This kind of poetry sees human sexuality as part of the earth's cycle of birth and death. "Earthy" is a perfectly accurate description of this kind of writing.

Here are two examples:

> —see their dancing around the bonfire
> The association of man and woman
> In daunsinge, signifying matrimonie
> a dignified and commodious sacrament.
> Two and two, necessary coniunction,
> Holding eche other by the hand or the arm
> Which betokeneth concorde. Round and round the fire
> Leaping through the flames, or joined in circles,
> Rustically solemn or in rustic laughter
> Lifting heavy feet in clumsy shoes,
> Earthfeet, loamfeet, lifted in country mirth
> Mirth of those long since under earth
> Nourishing the corn. Keeping time,

Keeping the rhythm in their dancing
As in their living in the living seasons
The time of the seasons and the constellations
The time of milking and the time of harvest
The time of the coupling of man and woman
And that of beasts.

Is it my imagination, or is there something rather self-conscious and patronizing about this passage? The poet is paying homage to the ancient earth goddesses, the powers of fertility—but he feels no real awe of them, he feels rather superior. I doubt if he would think of his own sex-life in these terms. These rustic mates are little more than animals to him. Procreative mating has no natural numinous significance for him, he has to try to create it, and I think he fails. The next poem tries even harder.

As we live, we are transmitters of life,
And when we fail to transmit life, life fails to flow
    through us.
That is part of the mystery of sex, it is a flow onward.
Sexless people transmit nothing.
And if, as we work, we can transmit life into our work,
life, still more life, rushes into us to compensate, to
be ready
and we ripple with life through the days.
Even if it is a woman making an apple dumpling, or
a man a stool,
if life goes into the pudding, good is the pudding
good is the stool,
content is the woman, with fresh life rippling into her,
content is the man.

The poet seems to be trying to find some sort of link between the "making" function of sex and the fiery, distinguishing power he understood so well. I don't think he succeeds. You could hardly find two men more dissimilar than the authors of these two poems, yet both of them, faced with the fact of

140

human fertility, suddenly lose their touch. Their symbols are second-hand, their words are worn-out clichés, their attitude is patronizing. Both would probably have asserted hotly the reality of their belief in what they say in these poems, but the poems belie them. There is no sense of immediate experience, although the experiences they describe are real and vivid to those who know them. The communication of intuitive under-standing has failed.

At this point I have to make more explicit use of personal reactions, which were necessarily my only guide in this search. I was forced to wonder why something so fundamental in human life as procreation should seem unable to tap the springs of intuition and issue in poetry.

The more I thought about it the more it seemed to me that this curious paralysis of intuitive communication of the signi-ficance of procreation was at the heart of a baffling puzzle of our particular culture.

Why is it that illicit passion definitely seems more exciting than the fidelity of married love? In terms of daily living (get-ting a living, shopping, making the bed) it clearly isn't. A temporary liaison has different tensions and trials and pleasures from married ones, but they are neither greater nor smaller, yet it continues to be haloed in a spiritual glow that even experience of the reality cannot extinguish. There is negative evidence of this in the acreage of print occupied by pious writers in attempting to prove that the glow is illusory. Is this merely the result of the romantic movement? And even if it is, why did the romantic movement happen? Sex which is non-procreative (in intention if not in practice) seems to have acquired a numinous quality that procreative married love lacks. Yet it was not al-ways so, and in other cultures still isn't so. In ancient cultures human fertility was religiously linked to the divine fertility in creation and preservation of life on earth. We now *feel*, if not believe, that the two are at odds. At first sight this would seem to be a retrogression, a loss of something valuable.

Yet the understanding of the sexual act that emerged from the work of various poets in the earlier part of this chapter makes it clear that there is no retrogression, but a very significant step forward towards a goal which we have not yet reached. The awareness of the divine fertility in human sex which was expressed in the fertility cults of the ancient pagan religions belongs to the time before Christ, even if it survived and survives in cultures that have not encountered him. If this seems obvious we might take a look at the obvious.

If Christ is the turning point, the fulfilment of the ages and the "coming man" then there had to be a difference in the divine method of education before and after. The education of the human race at the pre-Christian stage could only be concerned with the flesh, in the Pauline sense of the confusing and limiting factor in human life. It was necessary for man to feel the hand of God right in his life, even in his confused, fearful and ignorant flesh. Hence the awe at the power of God apparent in human procreation, and the various rites which sought to exploit the divine properties of human sex.

The Jewish teachers were already feeling for something more, and were very suspicious of any sexual reference in the religious context. They were aware that, as a way to God, sex by itself was a dead-end.

This conviction was reinforced by the early Christian teachers, who were naturally intoxicated by the glory of the freedom of Christ which loosed the baptized from the servitude of the flesh. But after the apostolic period many "Fathers" and teachers were inclined to identify the flesh not merely with the selfishness and confusions of a fallen physical nature but with sex itself, even in marriage, not yet perceiving that the transformation in Christ is of the whole human person. All the powers of the baptized are to be sanctified—and so gradually set free from the confusing and ignorant, even if often inculpable, flesh. The vision of freedom from the demands of the flesh naturally led to a glorification of consecrated virginity.

Less happily, it led to a denigration (sometimes explicit, and always in the Christian "atmosphere") of married sexuality, although marriage must inevitably be the vocation of the majority of Christians.

The curious phenomenon of the ideal of romantic love as it developed in the twelfth century takes on, seen against this background, the character of a revolt against an attempt to confine the human spirit. The Christian culture had lifted man out of the stage where he could only hope to find God in the signs of the flesh. Christians had, as it were, tasted freedom—but most of them were being denied the fruits of that freedom because they were not called to a state of religious virginity. Since Christianity as they understood it refused them what they now longed for they sought it outside Christianity, in the ideal of selfless devotion to a human woman. This is epitomized in the myth of Tristan and Iseult, which follows so closely the pattern of mystical experience. This ideal sprang up in revolt against Christianity as then understood—but it was a revolt of Christians, of men demanding their birth-right, the *new* birth-right of the baptized, the right to aspire beyond the flesh.

So the old fertility myths lost their power, as they had to do, because they belong to the power of the flesh and of death which made symbolic link with the annual cycle of seasonal fertility of the land. A new myth took their place, one which corresponded well with the new aspirations of those who had received the freedom of the sons of God—but the myth inevitably grew outside the sphere of official Christianity. Hence the division and confusion in the minds of Christians. Those who were called to the state of virginity could perhaps manage to ignore this division, since the difficulty is (or can be) resolved in their own person. For the married Christian the division at the heart of the Christian life has become gradually worse and more agonizing during succeeding centuries. One tradition of Protestant Christianity tried to solve it by refusing to recognize the value or eschatological significance of religious virginity. This did away with the division, but only by as it were lowering the temperature of the whole Christian life and virtually denying the possibility of the mystical experience of God in this life. You can see the results of this attempt in Donne, and you can see it didn't work. There was still no effective links between normal, procreative sexuality and the Christian experience of regeneration. The two things had to exist side by side, without inter-reaction. Sexuality, even that blessed by marriage, was tacitly relegated to the Old Testament stage of spiritual development by the Protestant refusal of the sacramental title to the marriage contract, and although the Catholic Church continued to maintain that matrimony was a holy state its image in the total picture of the Christian vocation was still that of a concession to the weakness of the unregenerate flesh. No wonder that fervent Christians felt more psychologically at ease in the state of virginity. It is a depressing fact that almost all the married people who were later canonized were widows or widowers, or were unhappy in their married life. We have no accurate record of the feelings of fervent Christians about the sex act, but the indirect evidence goes to show that it was usually regarded as a humiliating necessity made tolerable by love for the marriage partner.

So sex, even a sacramental sexual relationship, was still left outside the area of human nature which might be expected to be transformed by the Christian experience. For Christians, intercourse was a duty, though a blessed and happy one, if possible, for the sake of procreation. Yet the persistence and final revival of the romantic ideal bears witness to the fact that the human spirit was unsatisfied with this relegation of the most important of human relationships to a pre-Christian limbo.

The romantic ideal is a genuine expression of the aspiration of the human spirit towards its true freedom. It was forced to develop outside the framework of Christianity because the churches would have none of it—although this does not imply that they were unaffected by it. But at the same time more and more Christians were becoming overtly dissatisfied by this deep rift in the fabric of Christian living. They felt the need to integrate procreative sexual activity into the Christian life. The farming mystique, the back-to-the-land fiascos among Christians and non-Christians alike, were a recognition that something was missing from human life in European culture. The middle-class simple-life ventures were partly part of what was really an unconscious attempt to revivify the fertility religions. But these seemed irrevocably dead for Christians, or post-Christians, because their function as prophecy and sign-post was no longer needed and they had no deeper meaning. Non-Christian cultivators of the nature-mystique thought that a "free" sexual morality must be part of the programme for freeing human nature from what they rightly considered to be a prison. This was a rationalized misreading of the intuitive significance of the movement, as well as a dead-end in itself, socially and individually. Christians did not include this element, but their approach was basically the same—the two poems about fertility which I quoted were by a Christian and a self-styled pagan, but their approach to procreative sexuality is the same—and dead as mutton.

Here, I think, is the difficulty: The experience of married sexual love, open to procreation, can give to the open, loving and courageous individual an intense awareness that this experience has a reference beyond itself, that it is part of the process of both liberation and, through it, of assent towards a higher kind of existence. If it is to fulfil its potential it must be capable of expression in a form in which it can be reflected upon, and communicated. Even the individual who undergoes the experience cannot grow by it unless there is some means of, as it were, transferring the understanding gained from one instance of the experience to other occasions, and also to other departments of life. And beyond the life of the individual there is the life of the community. Only when an experience is capable of being shared can it be enriched by the *aperçus* of many, and so bring a greater nourishment to the life of the individual.

The meaning of sexual intercourse is experienced at the intuitive level, and must then be expressed as language before it can be communicated. But the only language in which intuitive experience can be expressed is the myth. However varied the interpretation, however sensitive the mind of the writer or speaker, the myth-framework has to be there, and it always is there.

There are plenty of myths about procreation—probably more than about anything else. Yet, as I suggested, when Christian or post-Christian writers used them they communicated nothing but embarrassment. And I suggest that this was because for them these myths have served their purpose and were spiritually dead, whereas the myth of regeneration through passion was not dead, for it expresses a genuinely contemporary and Christian experience of a vital element in human life.

I think this is why the concept of Christian marriage for all its beauty has not come to life as an exciting ideal; it is part of the reason why birth-control has become popular even apart from economic necessity. The liberation from the demands of child-bearing (essentially prosaic) appeals to the ethos of love-as-passion, distinguishing, burnishing, renewing. Possibly this is why there has sometimes been an aura of smugness about the "good Catholic families" of the past, an Old Testament atmosphere that lacks the sense of joy and freedom that should characterize those who have died and risen with Christ. It is a rather depressing fact that so many of those who in the last few generations, reared large families of potential Christians did so in what seems to be an unchristian way. Very sincere Christian married couples have often suffered from a hidden sense of guilt because they are not virgins. In order to reassure themselves that they were in fact doing God's will in spite of not being virgins they had to have a lot of children. More and more —with the compulsive repetitiveness of Old Testament sacrifices, which were endlessly repeated because in themselves they had no redemptive power. The sexual life of such people was an attempt to convince themselves that they were exactly what they ought to be, according to a preordained (Old Testament) pattern. Each act of intercourse had to reinforce the image in each partner. In the woman, that of passive submission and willingness to bear unlimited children, no matter what the circumstances, and in the man that of a sort of archetypal Father, protective and generative. So there was generation but no regeneration, no distinguishing of personality, no impulse of ascent, for the experience was forced into a pattern which left no room for the transforming effect of the baptismal vocation. It was pre-Christian, though often admirable and beautiful.

The difficulty for Christians in understanding the whole significance of the sexual experience is that we have lacked a myth framework by which we might express our intuitive knowledge of it. One aspect of it—the distinguishing, individualizing, liberating purpose of it—we could and can express. Though the form is not a Christian one the idea it expresses is truly and gloriously Christian. The other aspect, that concerned with the ideal of married procreativeness, remained unexpressed and therefore failed to communicate at the intuitive level.

But the two poems quoted last both belong to the last generation. There are signs, recently, that we may be finding the myth pattern by which the inward meaning of procreative sexuality may be expressed and communicated, and so spring to life. What the last generation failed to find this one is finding, perhaps partly because this generation is freed from the necessity to procreate, but *can* do so, by deciding to.

Here are a few lines from a recent "pop" record, though from one of the groups that appeal to the more sophisticated pop fans. Life and love are expressed under the traditional image of the journey, and the ship for the journey is both old and new:

> Come let us build the ship of the future
> In an ancient pattern that journeys far

And this journey is described in terms of what would once have
been called "classical allusions". But the allusions here are to a
type of myth more ancient and less specific than the usual detailed references culled from a schoolboy acquaintance with
classical mythology. The myth is renewed, because it is re-
discovered by people who have no inherited income from the
traditional pagan myth, but have found buried treasure unexpectedly. Here, human fertility is a deep intuitive experience
of oneness with all of life. Sexual love is part of the coming
together of living things rediscovering their oneness, and
human conception expresses the openness to the future of
the movement of being "oned", as Juliana of Norwich called
it:

> Seasons they change but with gaze unchanging
> O deep-eyed sisters is it you I see?
> Seeds of beauty ye bear within you
> Of unborn children glad and free
> Within your fingers the fates are spinning
> The sacred binding of the yellow grain
> Scattered we were when the long night was breaking
> But in bright morning converge again.

How different from the self-conscious earthiness of an earlier
generation! One important difference is that the earlier poet
looked to the past, and saw it continuing, whereas the new poet
is concerned with the future, though he sees its roots in the
deep past, and celebrates both. The feeling of it has a hopefulness which can be called paschal. The long night does seem to
be breaking. In this new dawn married couples are discovering
procreation as both liberating and uniting. Another recent
poem expresses this movingly, telling of a couple haunted in
their house by sounds, voices and dreams, as of little boys.
They search, wondering if a child has been killed in the house
and buried secretly. They think perhaps they may

> discover
> A pile of dusty bones like charcoal twigs and give
> The tiny-sounding ghost a proper resting place
> So that it need not wander in the empty air.

But the search ends differently:

> No blood-stained attic harboured the floating sounds,
> We found they came in rooms we'd warmed with our life.
> We traced the voice and found where it mostly came
> From just underneath both our skins, and not only
> In the night-time either, but at the height of noon
> And when we sat at meals alone. Plainly, this is how we
>   found
> That love pines loudly to go out to where
> It need not spend itself on fancy and the empty air.

In both these poems there is a sense that human fertility, the act of procreating, is something people *make*, enter into, or discover —because they realize its meaning and want to know what it can reveal. They are not earthily absorbed in a cosmic pattern imposed by the necessity of their nature. They choose freely, there is a sense of challenge and decision and hope. This is a Christian kind of experience, even when the people concerned are not Christians at all. It is a paschal experience.

The problem of the spiritual significance of sex is in some ways more urgent and poignant for a woman, because men, in our culture, have easily managed to feel themselves independent of, and superior to their sexual lives. This ability is in fact a symptom of a fatal spiritual disease, but the victims do not regard it as such. Women suffer other spiritual diseases but seldom this one, unless they deliberately infect themselves, in the mistaken conviction (popular in the thirties) that to erect impermeable barriers between areas of experience is a proof of "maturity". The writer of this poem clearly feels no need to do so:

> The eyeless labourer in the night
> the selfless, shapeless seed I hold,
> builds for its resurrection today—
> silent and swift and deep from sight
> foresees the unimagined light.
>
> This is no child with a child's face;
> this has no name to name it by:
> yet you and I have known it well.
> This is our hunter and our chase,
> the third who lay in our embrace.

Later in the same poem come these two lines:

> This is the blood's wild tree that grows
> the intricate and folded rose.

And it ends:

> Oh hold me, for I am afraid.

Here is the authentic note of real vision, the awe of something greater than we can understand. It seems to complete and answer the unspoken question left in the air by the previous poem and to make explicit the hints in the one before.

With this poem as supporting evidence, but by no means relying on it, I come to the conclusion to which all my travelling among the preoccupations of poets finally led me.

We are Christians, it is therefore both stupid and dishonest to try to think things out as if this fact made no difference. Many of the confusions which arise between Christians and non-Christians do so because Christians talk as if their framework of thought were exactly the same as that of those who reject Christianity, with the addition of a few extras. When the extras refuse to fit in smoothly we try to file them down and fit them in by arguments designed to suit an anti-Christian intellectual system.

So, through all the debate about the place or regulation of sex in human life, about fertility control and about the purpose of marriage, Christians continue to talk as if Christ had not risen.

But, if Christ is not risen then is our faith vain. In particular, our attempts to make sense of sexual love and procreation are extremely vain. This is not so because the resurrection proves the divinity of Christ and therefore gives him the right to tell us how to order our lives, but because the risen Christ is "first-born among many brethren", who are destined to share in his glory, the glory of physical human body. "In my flesh I shall see God."

If we apply the fact of the resurrection to the understanding of the experience of sexual intercourse, suddenly everything begins to fall into place. Here is the myth-framework we need, the symbol by which we can express our understanding of personal intuitive experience.

Here is the *reality* of the myth of regeneration through love that recurs constantly in our literature, the myth of love-as-passion, that of Tristan and Iseult. But the Tristan myth embodied only one aspect of the mystery of sexual love, the distinguishing and liberating one. The paschal myth brings together both sides and makes a unity of them: the individual purification, with its eschatological significance, and the procreative one. The resurrection as a myth-pattern has of course long been used to express the understanding of the vocation of consecrated virginity, which is bound up with the paschal mystery. In the early Church virgins were often consecrated during the Easter Vigil, at the same time as the catechumens were baptized. Virginity points ahead to the life of the resurrection, but on all the baptized, married and virgin alike, the flesh still makes its claim, because we aren't dead yet, and death is the condition of glorification. Christ attained his glory by accepting fully the conditions of fallen human life, even to the point of death. He "had to die, and so enter into his glory". The myth of love-as-passion implies that the transforming effect of love comes about not by directly tackling and overcoming the circumstances which prevent the fullness of possession, but

151

precisely by submitting to them, and *so* entering into glory. Passion means suffering, undergoing, but undergoing willingly, and with a purpose in mind.

The purpose is final union in a glorified state, and death is the way there, as Christ was not able to be united with his people until he was glorified, and the way to that glory was through death.

For those, therefore, whose vocation is not consecrated virginity but consecrated sexual love, sexual union is part of this undergoing, this passion, in both senses which are really one. It has this significance not because it is unpleasant (which is an accidental, not an essential, quality of passion), but because it is a willing submission, with a purpose in mind, a kind of "death". The submission aspect of sex has, in the past, been thought of as a purely feminine thing, for the woman was regarded as the passive receiver of the man's active love-making. But whatever the sexual "division of labour" in particular unions (and the "passive female" superstition is fortunately on the way out) the submission referred to here is the common submission to the experience of desire, of love, finally of conception. Sex and procreation are things we can choose *not* to experience, but we cannot make them, they are "bigger" than those who experience them. In this sense we "submit" to them, and co-operate with them, willingly or not.

But the Christian passion, this shared, willing submission to the purpose of the flesh, is essentially different from a blind, purposeless submission to the unavoidable; it is different again from mere obedience under the law. We make the ship of the future, hopefully, because we want to, but it has an "ancient pattern". This is quite different from the fruitless though understandable attempt to break out of the servitude of the flesh either by despising and crushing it or by refusing to recognize its servile character and treating its impulses as in themselves liberating.

The understanding of sexual intercourse as a means of grace, a way to the integration of the personality here and also to its final transformation in glory, is essentially a Christian understanding. And only the context of the paschal mystery or myth relates sexual love and procreation. The link is shown to us in symbol at every Easter vigil. The candle, Christ, goes down into the water of death, and there fertilizes the womb of his bride the Church, so that she may conceive. And he rises beyond death, alive with the new life which he shares with her. In Christian marriage, husband and wife submit willingly to this "death" which expresses their love, but does so in a dark and secret way which they can never fully understand or control. This going down into darkness is generative. From it a new life begins. But at the moment of intercourse they don't know if conception has taken place. They are in darkness. This is the condition of making of the new life, this ignorance. Death is essentially an abandonment to ignorance, and intercourse is a kind of death. The differences between the Christian and non-Christian attitudes to sexual intercourse are the same as the differences between the Christian and non-Christian attitudes to final physical death. For the Christian, death is a willing sacrifice, offered to God in union with Christ's death, and with the promise of glory beyond. For the non-Christian, death is simply the inevitable end, to be accepted with what dignity and courage one can muster. It has no significance beyond itself. In the same way the non-Christian sees in sexual intercourse an expression of love, an exchange of pleasure, a distraction from the troubles of everyday life and in marriage a bond of unity and a means of growth together. But it has no reference beyond the lives of the couple, and when sexual desire dies, that's it, it's over. (Many non-Christians *do* see more in it than this, as they see more in death than an end, but when they do they are unconsciously making use of myths with a Christian background.)

For many Christians, sexual intercourse means no more than it does for non-Christians, for they keep this side of their lives

153

in a pre-Christian psychological compartment. The vision proper to Christians, however, sees it as a sharing in the paschal mystery.

Once we can see that we can see a lot of other things. We can see why the Catholic Church has felt uneasy about artificial contraceptives in spite of the compelling practical reasons for them, for identification with the paschal mystery requires submission to and co-operation with the conditions of human nature, not a frontal attack on them. We can also see why non-Catholic Christians, as well as non-Christians, have found the Catholic attitude incomprehensible if not downright wicked, even where the stark necessities of survival did not force the issue. They have seen clearly one part of the significance of intercourse which Catholics have consistently underrated—that part which is represented by the Tristan myth—and they have realized sooner than Catholics the transforming purpose of sexual love. Perhaps, now that many traditional Christians are able to recognize that their understanding of the spiritual significance of sexual intercourse has been one-sided and deficient, and therefore their view of marriage has been so too, they may be able to go on to rethink both, and present a balanced and Christian interpretation of sexual love in the light of the resurrection. As Christians, surely the resurrection is what we should be concerned to preach? No-one has ever been known to die in defence of the natural law, but thousands have died joyfully for their faith in the risen Christ, and they were willing to go to death for it because it gave a meaning to life. As Christians, we are wasting our time handing out philosophical arguments. They might have had some relevance in a pre-Christian culture, in our time they are meaningless. The experience of sexual intercourse in all its aspects makes complete sense, earthly and heavenly sense, in the context of the resurrection. The response of poets interprets the intuitive experience of the less articulate, and both find their meaning and fulfilment in the myth which is also a matter of direct and personal experience for many—the experience of the risen Christ.

6. The Experience of the Spirit

IF the Spirit speaks to the listening people of God in the events of history, as well as in Scripture, then a renewed search for the springs of Christian spirituality is probably the most urgent task placed by the Spirit before the renewed Church of our time. The visible Church is the listening people. It is not all the people who listen, but it is an identifiable collection of those people who are supposed to be listening to God and acting on what they hear, and who indeed have pledged themselves to do so—though in some cases rather casually, or with extensive reservations. The people must listen to the breathing of the Spirit, even if the message be only whispered, but at this time it rises even to thunder.

At any time in the history of Christianity it would be taken for granted that the personal pursuit of holiness, or the imitation of Christ, or the experience of the Spirit, are indispensable to the Christian life. The emphasis is different under these three headings, but all definitions of how Christians deepen and increase their personal dedication in faith assume that this is something which is to be done in the assembly of God's people, by virtue of incorporation in Christ, with all the others who share that membership, but it also takes for granted that this is a personal matter, in which each one must strive and search, often apparently alone. The task and its rewards may belong to the whole, but they also belong to each member. The need for holiness is not new, but it is being newly demanded, with renewed urgency.

In the past two centuries an emphasis on individual holiness at the expense of a sense of social and political responsibility was an easy refuge for good people who wanted to be Christians without rocking the boat too much. Who shall blame them? It is normal to accept the assumptions of one's time without question and to assume that what does not fit them must be suspect, or impossible, or wicked. The reaction in favour of Christian social and political commitment has been very violent. Some over-compensation was inevitable, but we have been too busy despising the meticulous observances, moral nit-picking and private charities of our immediate ancestors to observe with sufficient clarity the growth among the new, socially-concerned Christians of a self-righteous lack of any observances at all; a moral vagueness combined with a constant readiness to quarrel about morality, and substitution of indignation about the State's failures of charity for any personal effort of love. Naturally this is not true of all, any more than Mauriac's religious *grenouilles* are a picture of typical French piety, even of the restricted milieu he portrays, but if we have been justified in castigating the mistakes of our precedessors in the job of being the Church we must make the effort to be equally ruthless about our own. This isn't easy, because the current prejudices are naturally the fashionable ones and nobody likes to be spiritually dowdy. Yet it is true that if those "old-fashioned" Christians (living in some vague period mistily associated with crinolines and fat prayer-books) were frequently guilty of private soul-cultivation as an excuse for public irresponsibility, we are too often guilty of irresponsible subjectivity in our private lives, not really compensated for by rather selective indignation in the public sector.

This is only one side of either coin and those reared in an "individualist" type of piety were frequently agonizingly aware of an element of built-in hypocrisy which could only be overcome by contradicting all the expectations that class, contemporary ethos and religious accommodation had built into the educational influences of the time. And this was a long time —the assumption that the basic Christian concern was personal salvation and personal holiness developed from the counter Reformation, but only became an axiom in the eighteenth and nineteenth centuries. Also we must remember that compensating enthusiasm for the missions, throughout. The efforts made by good people to live as Christians within a complex of un-Christian social and political edifices which they could not pull down without crushing themselves and all that they valued, should not provoke our contempt, but rather an admiration of the Spirit that did not surrender entirely in an apparently hopeless struggle. It is easy to see when an experience of the Christian life was limited and often defeated by false social and religious assumptions. It is less easy to recognize the extent to which sincere Christians refused to succumb to their social conditioning. But the effort is required of us. The effort is needed because the strength of that refusal is exactly commensurate with the strength and genuineness of their piety and the same measure applies to our own powers of resistance. To put it extremely simply, the holier individual Christians were, the more they resisted the destructive doctrines of their time, even though this resistance was often "instinctive" and combined with the normal acceptance of social structures and attitudes which we now recognize as destructive.

From many possible examples one typical experience of this resistance comes from the American foundation of the Society of the Holy Child Jesus, whose foundress was determined that the children of poor families should be taught, and the way to do this was to earn a living by educating the children of wealthy ones—who badly needed evangelizing anyway. This group of women, mainly from conventional middle and upper-class English homes, had been offered a "luxurious frame-house with a productive farm" for their first home in America. Their wealthy "patrons" dumped them in what turned out to be a leaky, half-rotten house in an overgrown jungle of garden. They had no money, scarcely any furniture and they were also short of blankets in the bitter cold of the draughty, unheated

157

house in a New England winter. They lived mostly on "pea soup" which "was only greenish water with a pea or two at the bottom of the bowl". They repaired the house as well as they could, endured the cold and hunger cheerfully, opened (and immediately filled) a village school in an ex-carpenter's shop and managed to recruit enough paying pupils for the school in the house itself (Catholic *and* Protestant, please note) to keep the village school open and avoid absolute starvation. Their pupils went on begging expeditions to local farms. The Sisters remained "gay and hard-working". Eventually, after a move, they won through and matters improved. But this kind of spiritual toughness and sense of priorities was not a matter of luck, or "breeding". It was the direct result of the type of the Christian formation which these young women had received from the foundress, and that was a result of Cornelia Connelly's own growth in the experience of the Spirit. At a time when the ecclesiastical passion for centralization and detailed control by long established codes was serving to prevent responsiveness to actual and present needs, she had to fight desperately for a Rule which stressed personal dedication and love, when a well-meaning Bishop tried to impose one that was almost wholly obsessed with administrative detail. Mother Connelly's work survived, as her own serenity and courage survived scandal, false accusations, illness, petty-minded officials and jealous colleagues. Her formation of her Sisters was based on the single-minded gift of oneself which her whole life exemplified, and which for her was summed up in a prayer of St. Francis which she copied down: "There is nothing on earth that I am not ready to abandon willingly with my whole heart, nothing—however painful—that I am not willing to endure with joy, nothing that I am not willing to undertake with all the strength of body and soul for the glory of my Lord Jesus Christ." Among the things she abandoned were a very happy family life, for which she has often been blamed since by those with a different experience, and with it the approval of her friends and relations. When she was asked to educate girls she rejected the obvious and refused to adopt the medieval-type education then normally offered to upper-class Catholic girls, tinged with deep suspicion of any intellectual achievement and devoid of any practically useful training either.

Cornelia had a passion for Christ, and therefore a passion for truth, which was stronger than her personal faults and which she managed to pass on to her spiritual daughters. She shared this passion with others who, in their time and place, found the strength and lucidity of mind to see through the prejudices and distortions of their time, and get to work in a setting conditioned by these, without despair and without bitterness. Matteo Ricci, Benedict Joseph Labre, Thérèse Martin, Philippine Duchesne, John Bosco, Bernadette Soubirous—the list goes on, and these few are only the Catholics on a list that extends across denominational boundaries, and includes such people as Elizabeth Fry, General Booth and Gladys Aylward. These wildly disparate characters had one thing in common: an originality and truthfulness of mind which sprang, perhaps, from natural genuis but which found its drive and staying power solely in the love of God. They made mistakes and sinned, and their mistakes and sins were often serious and often were typical of their time. They had the blindnesses of their time, but they also had a vision which mattered more.

There were others who tried to do good, and to serve God in all kinds of work, that obviously needed doing, but the story of each of the ones who had the real vision shows the way in which bright ideas, strength of mind, zeal and courage were not enough when holiness was lacking. Over and over again, the great threat to the enduring work of the people with a real passion for Christ has been the presence of other people with a passion for the image of themselves as servants of Christ. Here is another example of the way in which a genuine theology must judge experience, as experience makes theology grow.

This is where we came in. The real failures of our ancestors lay not in the limitations of their social and political vision, their narrow categories of virtue and of sin, and their baroque pieties, but in their lack of that single-minded sensitivity to the experience of the Spirit which could transcend these things. Our failure is likely to be as great or greater, if we allow ourselves to suppose that because we have been forced to become aware of categories of political and social sin to which they were insensitive we can rely on an accuracy of moral judgement which will infallibly guide our efforts in the right direction and ensure their success, or assure us that if they don't succeed that is the fault of the "opposition", which is, as infallibly, evil. Our moral failures are likely, in fact, to be considerably sicker than those of our forefathers, just because we can see further. Knowing so much, we are sure we know all, and refuse to consider that we might have our blind spots too. Knowledge without love or humility looks like being the death of the race, and it will certainly be the death of the Spirit in the race. The remedy lies where it always did—in the full growth of that Spirit through the following of Christ by each Christian.

As so often happens, the Church, the listening people, is being reminded of this truth by influences and signs in the world around. One of these signs is the growth of a real folk-song movement, very different from the middle-class cultivation of folk-arts of the thirties, though owing much to those "cranks" who got nowhere in their own time. All over the West, louder and louder through the monotoned rival incantations of the secular planners, whether of right or left, who treat the people as a lump to be forced into the correct shape of health and prosperity, rise the voices of the folk singers, in pubs and clubs singing songs of sorrow and marriage, birth and death, pain and joy, bawdry and bitter grief. They are songs about real, individual people living as human beings do, painfully, enjoyably and hopefully, and always searching. Funny, tragic, or wild, new ones and old ones, the songs all have this tone of nostalgia and hope, which is the tone of the human spirit that will not be reduced to a part of the mass, but is fiercely individual *because* it belongs to the whole people. The "folkness" of folk songs lies in just this—that they belong to all people by being about separate and unrepeatable and often very peculiar individuals. The struggle to be human is for each, but can only be sustained because each knows and celebrates the common humanity as he experiences it. It is this earthy spirituality that Christians need to recover if the Church is to be prophetic, wild, and holy, and not merely socially enlightened—necessary (and overdue) though that enlightenment may be.

There are other signs that it is time to take the lid once more off the well of truth from which the mystics and saints drew. The hopes of earlier decades that the right political philosophy would infallibly lead to justice and happiness have faded, because it was forgotten that man as a political animal is not less a spiritual one, and can be as good or as evil as he chooses, not as his ideology proposes. The reaction among some of the young in the direction a philosophy of anarchy is, when a Christian analysis is applied to it, a reassertion that the goodness of a society depends on the holiness of its members, which is released by love, not by regimentation, however kindly. Attempts to put such a philosophy into practice may not succeed for long, but the attempt itself is the kind of reminder we need that the springs of the Spirit are in people, not in the necessary political structures, though those structures are absolutely required, and required to be conformed to the needs of the Spirit, if the Spirit is to get things done. We no longer need to be told that the wrong social and political structures can suppress it—for a while—or deflect its course underground, but even a Church that has broken through old barriers to more democratic and flexible types of organization, carefully suited to the needs of the time, can soon be as empty and profitless as the old Cunarder *Queen Elizabeth*, if they are not lived in by people who know how to live.

Signs are all around us, in the hunger for spiritual space and

F

adventure that expresses itself in eccentricity of dress, in the rejection of luxury, technology and even cleanliness by people who are groping desperately for fresh air in a stiflingly materialistic world. Signs are present in the new primary schools, where children pursue, with only the necessary minimum of guidance, the study they have discovered for themselves, alone or in groups, and where the discipline and order spring from the demands of the work rather than of the teacher. Negative signs are there also, in the cult of sex which is not earthy and bawdy but despairing and clinically purified of passion and human grief and the wrestling with death. This is what happens when people cease to hope for the Spirit, or are afraid of it. Signs are there in the distortion of values which regards physical or mental weakness as sufficient to exclude the old, or the unborn, from the category of useful humanity, because usefulness is measured in terms of the ability to hold down a job or enjoy the more obvious pleasures of life. It is a calculation of value from which the power to give, or to inspire, love has been excluded. It is an ethos that would regard as a pathetic and disgusting waste of valuable time and energy the Sunday afternoons of one father who regularly wheels out his small son, whose grotesquely enlarged skull contains a brain incapable of response to any stimulus whatever.

But the perception of reality that can justify actions of the kind done by this father is one that grows on the edges of mystery, where people live in daily and conscious fidelity to the contradictions that underlie all human life. They know without being told that to abandon that commitment to unknowing is to destroy the basis of living. This strange loyalty is beautifully expressed in a poem by Jon Silkin on the death of a mentally defective son at the age of one. I can quote only a small part:

> Something has ceased to come along with me.
> Something like a person; something very like one.
> And there was no nobility in it
> Or anything like that.

Something was there like a one year
Old house, dumb as stone. While the near buildings
    Sand like birds and laughed
    Understanding the pact
    They were to have with silence.

This was something else, this was
Hearing and speaking though he was a house drawn
    Into silence, this was
    Something religious in his silence,
    Something shining in his quiet. . . .

As in the exploration of the spiritual meaning of sexuality, the
poet finds words for an experience that he shares with many
who are inarticulate. Yet they go on living by their experience,
drawing on a depth of humility and courage.

They often do it without knowing why, without support and
against opposition and contempt. But for the Christian, this
perception of mystery is central, it is explicit in the argument
of the cross, but it can only be interiorized by the personal
living of the whole situation, not by attempts to apply the
wholeness of the cross/resurrection insight into what life is,
analytically to situations of which our awareness is necessarily
partial because acquired by observation and reason, not directly.
The application of a Gospel ethic to our particular setting is
valid, but not sufficient, unless both are seen, and experienced,
and spoken, by people who walk the edge of that heart-
breaking mystery as their daily path.

It is not enough, even, to use awareness of the "edge" as a
kind of touchstone of realness. One of the signs raised by the
Spirit is the search in the arts for a way to undo the bonds that
normally tie human minds to a sequence of events they can
observe but not alter, and to plunge people into a "pure"
humanness. Some contemporary poets, dramatists and musicians seem to be trying to push us into this mystery, by denying
the reason any foothold, yet demanding its desperate exercise

in a finally useless attempt to take hold of an essential experience which is constantly offered yet never accessible. *Waiting for Godot* has become a sort of symbol/example of this. It seems like an attempt to humiliate the human confidence in the senses and in arguable conclusions to the point at which it will surrender its autonomy and consent to lie still and listen. Yet there is no peace here, because the reason for trying to force people to surrender their control is a rational type of despair, leading logically to a more final despair, not to the self-abandonment of love which trusts where it cannot see. Contemporary art says, "Let go, your attempts to make sense are the creations of a deluded self-confidence," but the Christian demand says, "Let go, and allow the things you obscurely want, and know, and the actions they impel you to which you cannot justify, to modify the sense you make."

To quote someone infinitely better qualified to speak than I am, Dan Berrigan in the article printed in the October 1970 issue of *New Blackfriars*, asks what we Christians are to do with our lives, in a world in which "day after day, people are seeing more clearly the dead-end character of the lives they are being required to lead, according to the canons of public policy and private decency". Seeing the signs already described, and others, and seeing that "politicians, churchmen, judges, punishers and rewarders and guardians of values and properties, [are] nearly all of them moving in the wrong direction, acting on the wrong diagnosis . . ." what can we do? And since he is a Christian, and therefore committed to walking on the edge of mystery, not in stoical recklessness but in love, he breaks out with an almost Pauline cry of trust in life through death: "What might we not create for the future, if we somehow see this period through, live in the breach, consent to be cut down to size, as only the imprisoned or the hunted are cut down, are forced to confront our poverty and wretchedness? . . . One must not waste so precious an opportunity." But the opportunity is not to be seized by accident or good luck. "In order to bring

THE EXPERIENCE OF THE SPIRIT

such things to pass, it is of first import, I would think, to be able to pray." That, with Jesus, who was "never quite respectable. He could not be academicized out of existence—there were always those ragged fools somewhere at the back of the mind, those literalists, fundamentalists really, urging on the ancient clumsy game. Hidden Springs, Saints. Subjects of awe, declamations, feast days, the Big Ones, almost (never quite) dead; better off dead. But never quite." Never quite. The list goes on, and includes typical literalists, Abbé Pierre, Dorothy Day—Dan Berrigan.

What about us, the bystanders, the ones who haven't (as least not yet) been dragged through a hedge backwards, perforce leaving behind the clutter of intellectual and moral trinkets, the sloganed buttons with which we convince ourselves that we are really involved? Do we have to wait for God to ruffle our hair and cover us with leaves and ridicule before we consent to be "cut down to size" and rediscover the literal Jesus of the saints? In that case there is no Church but only a club for geniuses. What the folk-songs are saying, and the junk-shop finery in the demonstrations, and the absorbed six-year olds covered in clay, and the angry poets who miss the still centre, and the father wheeling his idiot son through the park, is that there is a Church, full of people each of whose job is holiness—being with Jesus—without reserve, often without full understanding, but also without the kind of spiritual evasiveness pretending to be humility that leaves the battle to the giants.

There are no bystanders in this war. Thomas Merton was wrong when he felt, in the introduction to one of his last books, that his monastic commitment made him "inevitably something of a bystander". His own life was a proof that it did no such thing, and his life and work deprives the rest of us of excuse for standing by.

But it is easy to say, and even to see, that the war against principalities and powers allows no civilians. It is not so easy to see where we get started in training. Or, to abandon the

165

Pauline metaphor (it is perhaps a little too near the bone) how do we set about finding the spring of true contemplation, holiness, which should well up in the baptized but is so easily drained off into marshes of self-deception and worldliness (the best butter, of course)? We cannot copy our forefathers, because we think and feel differently, we are a different kind of people. The old books, and the old advisers, tried to show us how to seek for holiness wherever we might be, on the assumption that we had to stay there, or at least that there was not normally any necessity for us to go anywhere else. We know, now, that we nearly always do have to go "somewhere else" to seek holiness, at least in the sense of a drastic shift in accepted values and way of life. The world that drove Dan Berrigan underground, and finally into goal, is not a world that allows Christians to grow in Christ, placidly, in the bed where heredity or natural ability or chance, planted them. Yet we have to start from where we are, and discover where to go because the Spirit pushes us. And we become aware of the pushes by the habit of openness to God and man, in prayer, as Dan Berrigan said.

There is plenty to be said about that, but not by me. Growing from that, as the tree grows from its roots (but the roots also need the light and air which the leaves collect) the decisions follow, in reaction to specific situations, but not pragmatically because they are decisions in the Spirit. What kind of decisions? Nothing very new. To give help where it is needed, not where it is easy; to resist the propaganda of evil, even when it is fashionable evil; to accept a lower standard of living even if it means being peculiar; not to wave the popular flag, even the popular Christian flag, when it is not obvious that it has a cross on it; or simply going on searching, and apparently staying still, and feeling unhappy about that, because God is still busy over private preparations of his own, and isn't in a hurry to show the way to go.

In all these ways we shall follow in the steps of our fathers, but in order to do so we may perhaps have to cling more closely than they did to the edge of mystery. Our way is certainly not harder but it is more problematic. The old path of personal self-discipline and deepening prayer is still there, but it can too easily take a detour around the less personal and immediate responsibilities of being here and now. People who feel the wind of the Spirit but don't recognize whose breath it is escape this difficulty sometimes by the search for a purely passive type of spirituality which lets them off confronting the political agonies of the time. The escape in the opposite direction is to identify with these and so avoid confronting the evil at the roots of the world. But the Spirit is the Spirit of Jesus, and neither way out will do for him, but only the intersection of time and eternity which is the cross. Which, means, at least in part, doing without the satisfaction of knowing what one is at, because it is not entirely oneself that is at it. *C'est plus fort que moi*, and very much odder than any of us can hope to understand.

But if there is no leaflet of printed instructions issued for this job there are the signs to be considered, just as there are signs that show the acuteness of the need for a recovery of a genuine experience of the Spirit. These same signs show which way the wind is blowing. It is blowing in the direction of an idiosyncratic type of Christian holiness, out of step with the times yet meeting its obscurely expressed needs, and often out of step with the more orderly (and equally necessary) aspects of Christian life and Church. It is blowing away from the worship of technology, and will therefore make itself unpopular with the still prevailing (though attacked) ethos of the Age of Business. It brings especially a fresh breath of the voluntary poverty of the gospels, and of the discovery of brotherhood in comparatively informal ways. The results of a responsiveness to the new breathing of the Spirit are things like the new monastic life of Boquen where celibates, married people, permanent members and temporary ones, form one community in Christ; or like the older established groups in the houses of hospitality in New

York and in great city slums across the United States, where all share the food of the poor; or like the Simon communities and similar ones in England; or the even more drastically committed women who gathered round Mother Theresa in Calcutta to care for the most destitute, sick and abandoned of all. It has produced farming communes and draft-resisters and dedicated squatters and people like the Petits Frères who live and worship in tenement flats and work in factories. It has also produced, significantly, a small but useful crop of hermits.

This isn't a religious revival, which can be useful but can equally be quite spurious. This is the old routine of building the kingdom. The difference is that the kingdom of this world, after a period of looking like an impressive option for humanity, has once more turned out to be literally dust and ashes. But the other kingdom is not made with hands, or not just hands. The kingdom of heaven is within you, which means, for most of us, that we need cracking open.

For if there is one lesson that emerges from the study of the varieties and forms of Christian experience it is that a truthful theology requires a truthful expression of experience. Like the poets, we need to have the "ability and willingness to face the full range of (our) experience with full intelligence; not to take the easy exits of either the conventional response or choking incoherence". But the spiritual integrity and sensitivity required of the Christian is more far-reaching than that of the poet, because it has to prepare him not only to face experience fully but to take decisions on the basis of that experience, as he interprets it in the light of the gospel. And these decisions not only commit the individual, but the sum and tendency of them commits the whole people, truthfully or not. Theology has to be the result of the whole Church reflecting on its experience, and the theology will be true to the Spirit of Christ when, and only when, it is the poetry of a holy people.